PLEASING GOD:
THE JESUS AGENDA

Christian Priorities and Politics

By
HERSCHEL HILL

PLEASING GOD: THE JESUS AGENDA
By Herschel Hill

Dreamervision Publishing
225 W. Ashland Ave., Suite 2
Indianola, IA. 50125
www.dreamervision.com

Printed in the United States of America

ISBN 978-0-9786553-8-9

LCCN - 2007942505

Also by Herschel Hill

Looking Toward Eternity: A Life Hereafter?

America, A House Divided

"The Spirit of the Lord is on me, because he has anointed me to preach good news to the poor. He has sent me to proclaim freedom for the prisoners and recovery of sight for the blind, to release the oppressed, to proclaim the year of the Lord's favor."

Luke 4:18-19 NIV

CONTENTS

A Word from the Author

Christians claim to be the family of God, joint heirs in Jesus Christ His Son, bound together in love for God and love for one another, under the Lordship of Christ, guided by the indwelling Holy Spirit, and committed to carry on the redemptive work of Christ in our world today. Yet, I see individual Christians, local churches, denominations, and the Christian community as a whole squabbling over theology, church doctrine, worship practices, ideology, and controversial moral and social issues. Close ties between the religious right and the Republican Party, a mixing of religion and politics, has created a volatile political climate in America. I cannot believe God desires such fighting among His people.

Christian entities are getting more and more involved in secular politics. They have chimed in with hateful political rhetoric, slanderous and misleading political ads, character assassination, and other divisive actions normally associated with secular politics. Respect for religious leaders and Christianity as a whole is on a downward spiral because of the words and antics of some in the Christian community. And, many of our Christian leaders have been found guilty of embezzlement, sexual abuse of workers and minors, marital infidelity, and fraud and corruption. Needless to say, such conduct by Christians, especially by our leaders, has a negative impact on our witness for Jesus Christ.

We are told throughout the Bible to love our neighbor. That means putting away attitudes of disrespect, favoritism, self-righteousness, judgment, and animosity toward those we disagree with. God's Word tells us to treat others, including our enemies, with respect, compassion, mercy, justice, and love. The Old Testament and the New Testament command us to take care of and stand up for poor, weak, sick, oppressed, and helpless people in our society. That was a major thrust of Jesus

Christ's personal mission on earth, and it is an integral part of Christians' calling to carry on Jesus' work.

Too many Christians spend their time and resources fighting over controversial and divisive moral and social issues rather than addressing the social ills afflicting our citizens today. The Christian community must heed the Biblical mandate to minister to the needs of the helpless people in our midst who cannot help themselves. God is a champion of the downtrodden, thus I believe a compassionate social ministry to the needy in our society and around the world is more pleasing to Him than fighting among ourselves over controversial moral and social issues.

My goal in this book is to define Christian priorities pleasing to God. Join me as we humbly and prayerfully turn to God's Word for guidance.

Herschel Hill

Chapter 1

Diverse Christian Priorities

America is considered to be a Christian nation, but that does not mean we are a people with uniform religious beliefs and practices. One has only to look at the bickering between Christian denominations and the strife within denominations to see the religious diversity in our country. Numerous Christian organizations are also heavily involved in secular politics, and the differences in their religious views are amplified in the political arena. Factor in the beliefs and practices of rapidly growing non-Christian religions in our nation, together with the views of those citizens free of any religious affiliation, and the degree of diversity becomes enormous. So, how can America, a predominately Christian nation, best please God? How can the wide variety of religious entities, some involved in politics and some not, express their beliefs and practice their religions without infringing on the constitutional rights of other citizens?

Christians in our country are arbitrarily divided into two basic groups. One group is labeled conservatives with right-wing beliefs, whereas the other group is classified as liberals with left-wing views. Obviously, many Christians fall in the middle; they do not ascribe to either view, they lean slightly left, or they lean slightly right. The more vocal voices of the extreme right and the extreme left, however, tend to mute the moderate voices of the middle. Extreme conservatives are often referred to as fundamentalists, or the religious right.

Christianity in America thus encompasses a wide spectrum of religious beliefs and practices. Fundamentalist conservatives represent one end of the spectrum, and extreme liberals occupy the opposite end. Individual religious entities within that range determine their particular core beliefs, methods of exercising their faith, their relationship with the overall Christian community, and their involvement in secular affairs and politics. A large number of Christian organizations are heavily involved in our nation's politics, whereas others are not. That means some churches, denominations, and similar religious organizations are more active than others in addressing a multitude of moral, social, and political issues in our country. Their priorities and political involvement may vary, but each Christian entity seeks to carry out what they perceive to be God's purpose for them. Oftentimes, their perceived mandates lead to encroachment into the political realm.

The United States Constitution and accompanying Bill of Rights form the foundation upon which our country is founded. Unfortunately, many of our citizens cannot agree with one another regarding interpretation of those basic documents, especially the First Amendment to the Constitution.

> Congress shall make no law respecting an establishment of religion, or prohibiting the free exercise thereof; or abridging the freedom of speech, or the press; or the right of the people peaceably to assemble, and to petition the government for a redress of grievances.

The first part of that Amendment, the portion dealing with religion, has been particularly troublesome. A large number of Christians, especially the religious right, interpret that clause to mean freedom of religious expression in any place at any time, even in public schools and government facilities. That interpretation enables them to justify state-sponsored prayer in public schools, posting the Ten Commandments in government buildings, and teaching the Biblical account of creation (intelligent design) in public school science classes.

On the other hand, more moderate Christians believe the First Amendment prohibits the outward expression of religion in such public forums because it imposes one's religious beliefs and expressions on others. They interpret religious freedom to mean freedom of religion and freedom from religion. That view is known as separation of church and state, and it is a view which for the most part has defined our nation's history. Recent court decisions have also supported separation of church and state, but those judicial rulings have not stopped the heated debates and wrangling over the freedom of religion issue. That hot-button issue is the basis for much of the division gripping our country, and it has spread into the political realm of our nation.

America is a bitterly divided country, and the two opposing political factions attack one another continuously with animosity and abusive rhetoric. And, that conflict is taking place in what we claim to be a Christian nation. My previous book, *America, A House Divided,* identified and discussed at great length primary sources of the polarization gripping our great country. We are burdened with an extremely partisan political system; lobbyists with deep pockets corrupt our politicians and our government; divisive religious fundamentalism has entered the political arena; politicians are essentially bought by wealthy special-interest groups; abuse of the environment by corporations and business interests is widespread; slanderous and untruthful political ads saturate news outlets; and a disastrous war in Iraq intensifies the polarization of our people.

All of those factors and others are somewhat related, and they all involve politics to some extent. Religious fundamentalists, or the religious right, have attained a dominant position in the Republican Party, so virtually all the controversial issues in our society are affected to some degree by religion. That blending of moral, social, and political issues has created an environment in which our citizens relate to one another with animosity and contempt rather than with love and respect. That should not be the norm in a Christian nation like America. How can individual citizens, and our country as a whole, be more pleasing to God in today's complex and divided society? The primary focus in this book is to find an answer to that difficult question. The religious right is heavily involved in the political realm of our country, so a secondary goal is to determine if both the religious right and their political opponents are following Biblical guidelines as they squabble over controversial moral and social concerns. The purpose of this book is not to determine which side is right or wrong on all individual moral and social issues. Instead, our goal is to assess, and hopefully change, the way the two sides relate to each other on the issues. We endeavor to meet that goal by applying Biblical teaching to the attitudes and actions of our people.

People of faith hold a wide range of beliefs with regard to Christians' perceived mandate from God for their role in our society. One large segment, quite often referred to as the religious right, places major emphasis on religious, moral, and social issues such as abortion, euthanasia, homosexuality, gay marriage, state-sponsored prayer in public schools, teaching of creationism in public school science classes, posting the Ten Commandments in public buildings, use of embryos in stem cell research, and similar social conservative causes. They are passionate about those issues and they are very active politically. The religious right also strives to incorporate their particular beliefs into the laws of our land and policies of our government.

Other Christians with more moderate religious views place a higher priority on eliminating social injustices, helping the weak and powerless in our society, protecting our environment, standing up for the downtrodden in our midst, providing equal opportunities for education and health care, eliminating discrimination, and other similar social issues. Moderate Christians are equally fervent in their efforts to address all those social ills afflicting our nation. The primary thrust of our study is therefore to determine what God really wants from His people. Does God want His people to pursue the social conservative agenda of the religious right, or does He desire that we address the social ills prevalent throughout our country and around the world? Join me as we seek an answer to that difficult question.

Clearly, a significant number of non-Christian citizens of our nation support both the political and moral agenda of the religious right and the broader social agenda of moderate Christians. Our study, however, is directed primarily at the attitudes and agendas of the religious right and moderate Christians. We must recognize though that both factions are comprised of sincere and committed people of faith striving to please God. Their religious, moral, and social beliefs, together with their actions, are guided by their interpretations of the Bible, God's Word. So, rather than trying to prove which side is right or wrong on specific issues, our focus is to determine how our country can best please God. In other words, what should America's priorities be with regard to controversial religious, moral, and social issues?

Let us remember as well that all Christians share important commandments from the Bible. For example, each of us is told in Scripture to be actively involved in evangelism, the sharing of the Gospel of Jesus Christ, the Good News, with a lost world. That sharing of the Good News is demanded of all Christians. We spread the Gospel by means of verbal communication of both our faith and the Good News to others, and by means of our living witness, the way we live our lives. The way we live our lives and relate to other people are thus extremely important. That is a prime consideration as we attempt to identify attitudes and actions that are most pleasing to God.

Committed Christians across the religious spectrum cling to strong beliefs concerning what they perceive to be moral issues. A sizable number of our citizens, including both conservative Christians and more moderate Christians, consider drinking alcoholic beverages to be a sin. On the other hand, other Christians deem moderate use of alcohol, or social drinking, to be acceptable. A subsequent chapter of this book is devoted to that controversial topic. There is also widespread disagreement among Christians regarding various other religious and moral issues. Some members of the overall Christian community regard either moderate gambling, dancing, wearing jewelry and makeup, working on Sunday, retail sales on Sunday, or other such activities as sinful conduct. A majority of Christians, however, disagree with each of those views. God's people cannot even agree on a fundamental issue such as tithing. Faithful and dedicated Christians hold to diverse beliefs regarding the necessity to tithe and the required amount to tithe. The way Christians relate to one another over those controversial issues is of prime importance. Do we relate to those with whom we disagree with love and tolerance, or do we view the opposing side with animosity and a judgmental attitude?

Our attitude toward others, especially those with whom we have differences of opinion, is of utmost importance. Too many times, we are perceived by others as self-righteous, judgmental, and condescending. Such a holier-than-thou attitude toward fellow citizens does not gain the respect of those with whom we disagree and certainly does not please God. And, anything that displeases God must be called sin. Much more will be said about wrong attitudes in later chapters of this book. The Old Testament clearly defines God's desired attitudes and actions for His chosen people, the Jews. The New Testament clarifies, expands, and applies Old Testament teaching to Christians, God's universal church. Included in the New Testament are Jesus' instructions to us and His example for us. As God's people, we would do well to imitate the attitudes and actions of Jesus.

Greed and corruption permeate secular life in America today, and that culture of greed and corruption has moved into the religious realm as well. Our local, state, and national governments are plagued with widespread corruption, and many of our politicians, Christian and non-Christian alike, are controlled by greed. We see and hear about corruption in our nation's business community, and unethical and illegal behavior characterizes a significant number of our business leaders. Individual citizens are no better. Greed for wealth, power, and prestige is evident in the lifestyle and conduct of many Americans today. Sadly, we see the same high level of greed and corruption in the religious community. Churches, church leaders, and individual members are quite often controlled by the same desire for wealth and power that drives the secular world. Many Christians emphasize the Bible's teaching with regard to specific moral issues but ignore the same Bible's instructions and admonitions against greed and corruption. Such selective obedience to God's Word cannot be pleasing to Him.

In the Book of Genesis in the Old Testament, humankind is given dominion over the whole earth. That includes all animal life and plant life, the ground upon which we walk, the air we breathe, the water we drink, and all the earth's other resources. God provided all those things for our benefit and for our use. God also made humankind caretaker of His creation. That means we are responsible for preserving, maintaining, and protecting our environment and for the sensible use of the earth's resources. Abuse and misuse of the environment is the norm for our society today, quite often by Christian business leaders and individuals who profess to be obedient to the Word of God. Could it be that such unconcern for the environment is the result of selective adherence to the teaching of Scripture?

Our stated goal in this study is to determine how America can best please God, but we see a Christian community clinging to a wide range of opinions about what God desires of His people. Our study results are thus dependent on significantly different interpretations of Scripture by various religious entities. So how do we factor in those differences in Bible interpretation? Sincere and committed Christians study the Bible and come away with diverse beliefs regarding what the Bible teaches about controversial moral and social issues. We must account for those inconsistencies in Scripture interpretation if we are to determine accurately how Christians, and our nation as a whole, should set priorities to deal with critical religious, moral, and social concerns. Let us establish what I consider to be sound Bible study guidelines as we endeavor to interpret key Scripture passages and apply them to some of the controversial moral and social issues prevalent in our society.

The Scripture passages utilized in this study are from either the New International Version (NIV) of the Bible or the New American Standard (NAS) Bible. The truth and authority of the quoted Bible passages are without question, but the views, comments, and conclusions included herein represent the author's interpretation and understanding of Scripture. You, the reader, most likely disagree with a number of the views and interpretations expressed by the author, and you assuredly have differences of opinions with other readers on some topics. When we have such a disagreement or question about the meaning or application of a particular Bible passage, we turn to other passages for clarification. We let Scripture interpret Scripture. Many Bible passages are difficult to comprehend and apply without turning to other passages dealing with the same or related topics. Oftentimes, the context or application of an individual Scripture passage is not apparent until other passages are studied and compared to it. That is especially true when trying to determine the relative emphasis to place on different passages which address a variety of seemingly unrelated issues. I believe this approach to Bible study facilitates a more complete and a clearer understanding of the basic truths presented in Scripture.

Jesus Christ, the Incarnate Son of God, came into our world to provide a way to reconcile sinful humankind to Holy God. He gave His life on the Cross at Calvary to atone for our sins, but Jesus did much more. During His three-year earthly ministry, Jesus taught His disciples how His followers should live their lives and how people should relate to one another. Jesus' teachings, which are contained primarily in the Gospels of Matthew, Mark, Luke, and John, were recorded by men inspired by the Holy Spirit of God. That record of Jesus' teachings is what we refer to as the New Testament. Jesus also gave us an example to emulate in our lives. He ministered to the needs of those people He came into contact with, and He demonstrated love for all humankind, including His enemies as well as His friends. The love Jesus demonstrated toward all people, Agape love, is a selfless love which seeks what is best for the object of that love, regardless of cost to self. Let us keep in mind Jesus' teachings and His attitude and actions toward others as we strive to determine what God desires of our country.

Christians today must make every effort to obey the teachings of the Bible. God's word tells us how we should live our lives, how we should minister to those with various needs, and how we should strive to be Christian examples to people around us. Being a good Christian example and living an exemplary life undoubtedly lead to a positive influence on the world around us. But, does that mean we should try to change those individuals we perceive to have sin in their lives? Many fundamentalist Christians seem to believe they have a directive from God to change other people. I am not sure the Bible incorporates such a commandment, so that is one area to be considered carefully in a subsequent chapter of this book.

Baptists in America exemplify the theological, social, and political conflict that has characterized the Christian community. Northern and Southern Baptists split in the mid-1800s over the issue of slavery, and the Southern Baptist Convention (SBC) proceeded to become the largest Protestant denomination in our country. A major schism developed in the SBC about thirty years ago over theology. Fundamentalist conservative Baptists gradually gained control of the Convention, and moderate Baptists were purged from all leadership and decision-making positions. Over that same time period, the SBC became more and more involved in secular politics. First, the SBC was associated with the political agenda of the Moral Majority led by Jerry Falwell. More recently, they have been heavily involved in the Christian Coalition's political activities supporting the Republican Party. Today, the Southern Baptist Convention, together with other fundamentalist Christians, has achieved a dominant position in the Republican Party. They are at the forefront of the religious right's battles over hot-button issues such as abortion, gay marriage, gay rights, prayer in public schools, use of embryos in stem cell research, and other such moral and social issues.

Moderate Baptists recently initiated an effort to place a greater emphasis on compassionate social ministries in America and around the world. Moderate Baptists are no longer willing to allow the Southern Baptist Convention to continue as the self-proclaimed voice of all Baptists in our country. They are trying to divert attention away from the divisive theological and moral issues championed by the religious right. Moderate Baptists want to focus instead on issues that bind them together, the social concerns championed by Jesus in His teachings. In addition to evangelism, which is the primary thrust for all Baptists, they want to address widespread poverty and disease, social injustices, environmental abuses, racial oppression, unequal education and employment opportunities, and other similar social ills in our society.

Leaders from some forty Baptist organizations in North America met recently in the Carter Center in Atlanta, GA. That initial meeting was arranged by former President Jimmy Carter, with assistance from Bill Underwood, President of Mercer University. The result of that meeting was the birth of a new Baptist alliance, the New Baptist Covenant, a compassion-oriented ministry that places emphasis on cooperation rather than on divisiveness. Participants at that meeting included representatives from the North American Baptist Fellowship, the Cooperative Baptist Fellowship, the four largest African-American Baptist Conventions, three Southern Baptist State Conventions, Hispanic Baptist groups, Canadian Baptists, and other U.S.-based ethnic Baptist groups. A second meeting is scheduled in early-2008, with some 20,000 participants expected. It is anticipated that both Democrats and Republicans will participate in that second meeting to preclude partisan division. As expected, however, criticism of the new Baptist alliance is emanating from the Southern Baptist Convention's fundamentalist leadership, primarily because of the involvement of former President Bill Clinton in the new alliance.

The unanswered question in Baptist organizations, as well as in the overall Christian community, is, "What should Christians in America do to please God?" Fundamentalist conservatives seem to believe we should support the religious, moral, and social agenda of the religious right. That means continuation of the social conservative movement initiated about thirty years ago by the Moral Majority and now led by the Christian Coalition. Moderate Christians are convinced America should address the social ills afflicting our country. They believe the highest priority for Christians, other than evangelism, is to minister to the needs of the weak and helpless in our society, reduce injustices in our business and legal systems, provide equal opportunities for education and employment, ensure livable wages for all working people, make health care available for all our citizens, protect the environment, and other similar social concerns. It is not a matter of deciding which side is right and which side is wrong on individual issues. It is a matter of determining which overall agenda should be given the highest priority. That is what we are attempting to do in this study, so join me as we apply the teaching of God's Word to our society today.

Chapter 2

Agenda of the Religious Right

The religious right is comprised primarily of fundamentalist conservative Christians who share concerns and beliefs pertaining to controversial religious, moral, and social issues in our society. They are sometimes referred to as social conservatives, or the Christian Coalition. Hot-button issues addressed by the religious right include abortion rights, euthanasia, homosexual rights, gay marriage, state-sponsored prayer in public schools, teaching of creationism (intelligent design) in public school science classes, posting the Ten Commandments in public facilities, and using embryos in stem cell research. Those divisive issues have fueled the social conservative movement over the last thirty years.

We must recognize though that all fundamentalist conservatives do not support the religious right on one or more of those issues near and dear to them. For example, we find substantial disagreement within social conservative ranks regarding teaching of creationism in public school science classes and using embryos in stem cell research. In a like manner, not all moderate Christians oppose the religious right on each and every moral and social issue. Quite a few moderate Christians agree with fundamentalist conservatives on issues such as state-organized prayer in public schools and abortion rights. A sizable percentage of non-Christians agree with the religious right on a number of issues as well, whereas other non-Christians align themselves with moderate Christians on the same issues. We encounter a wide variety of divisive moral and social issues throughout our society; hence it is very difficult to identify a major segment of our citizenry in agreement on every single issue.

For purposes of this study, however, we identify the religious right as fundamentalist conservative Christians who are in general agreement on the controversial religious, moral, and social causes prevalent in our society today. Similarly, Christians opposed to the religious right are referred to as moderate Christians. We must not be overly concerned about the exceptions to those general classifications, because our study results will not be invalidated as a result of the rather limited diversity within the ranks of both the religious right and moderate Christians.

Social conservatives share strong and somewhat narrow-minded beliefs concerning divisive issues such as abortion rights and gay marriage, and they are intolerant of opposing views. The religious right is quite vocal and actively engaged in their causes, and they strive to incorporate their particular religious and moral beliefs into the laws of our land and the policies of our national and state governments. Fundamentalist conservatives maintain the Bible supports their views on controversial moral and social issues, thus they reject any compromise of their positions on those causes. Such a stance obviously leads to division within the overall Christian community. The religious right considers division in America over religious and moral beliefs to be a good-versus-evil struggle, and they place themselves on the side of good.

Conservative Republican politicians embraced social conservatives over the last twenty-five years and incorporated their beliefs and views into the Republican Party agenda. At the same time, the religious right adopted the Republican Party's policies and views regarding non-religious issues, including but not limited to, gun control, anti-affirmative action, tax policies, and school vouchers. Today, fundamentalist conservative Christians represent a sizable and integral part of the Republican Party, and the Christian Coalition has a tremendous influence on Republican Party policy. Social conservatives are an extremely committed and a very active constituency; hence they are major players in local, state, and national politics.

The foremost religious and moral issue for the religious right is abortion rights, a sanctity of life issue. Social conservatives oppose legalized abortions, and they work diligently to get the Roe v. Wade Supreme Court decision overturned. The battle over abortion is waged in Congress and the federal courts, at the state level, and at the local level. A major goal for the Christian Coalition is to win nominations of conservative judges to the United States Supreme Court so rulings allowing legalized abortion can be repealed. The Supreme Court is almost evenly divided now, with a five to four majority favoring abortion rights, so one additional conservative Supreme Court justice could tilt the scales in favor of the religious right.

We stated previously that the intent of our study is not to determine if social conservatives are right or wrong on the issue of abortion. Bible scholars, legal scholars, and the medical community have debated abortion rights for many years, and they have made little progress toward resolution of the matter. Our primary concern is the animosity and contempt with which the two sides relate to one another. Each side turns to the Bible to justify their position on the matter, although abortion is never mentioned in Scripture.

Pro-Lifers, the religious right, argue that one of the Ten Commandments, "You shall not murder." (NAS) and related passages in the Old Testament support their position on abortion.

> For thou didst form my inward parts; Thou didst weave me in my mother's womb. I will give thanks to Thee, for I am fearfully and wonderfully made; Wonderful are Thy works, And my soul knows it very well. My frame was not hidden from Thee, When I was made in secret, And skillfully wrought in the depths of the earth. Thine eyes have seen my unformed substance; And in Thy book they were all written, The days that were ordained for me, When as yet there was not one of them.
> --Psalm 139:13-16 NAS

Social conservatives interpret this passage in Psalm 139 to mean that the fetus in a mother's womb is a person from the time of conception. Taking that fetus' life, an abortion, thus constitutes murder. Pro-Choice adherents, those in favor of legalized abortions, do not agree with that interpretation.

A Scripture passage in the Book of Exodus seems to support moderate Christians, who believe that aborting a fetus is not the same as taking a person's life after he or she has been born.

> "And if men struggle with each other and strike a woman with child so that she has a miscarriage, yet there is no further injury, he shall surely be fined as the woman's husband may demand of him; and he shall pay as the judges decide. But if there is any further injury, then you shall appoint as a penalty life for life, eye for eye, tooth for tooth, hand for hand, foot for foot, burn for burn, wound for wound, bruise for bruise."
> --Exodus 21:22-25 NAS

This passage in Exodus was included in the Jewish "laws of retaliation," the prescribed punishment for those who caused loss or injury to others. If an injury to a pregnant woman resulted in a miscarriage, the loss of an unborn fetus, the penalty was an amount set by the woman's husband and approved by a judge. But if there was any further injury to the woman, other than the miscarriage, the penalty was life for a life, eye for an eye, tooth for a tooth, and so forth. Clearly, the loss of the fetus was not considered to be the same as loss of the woman's life. The implication is that the fetus is not a person until after birth. Social conservatives obviously disagree with that interpretation.

The Bible does not provide conclusive and clear-cut teaching concerning the abortion issue; hence we see diverse beliefs among sincere and committed Christians. Citizens in our nation have subscribed to three primary views on abortion rights. A large number of fundamentalist conservatives claim all abortions are prohibited by the Bible, regardless of circumstances surrounding the pregnancy. They therefore seek to pass laws making all abortions illegal. Another significant segment of our population believes abortions should be illegal, but with a few exceptions. They believe that abortions should be allowed in the event the pregnancy results from rape or incest, if carrying the fetus to term would endanger the life of the mother, or when the fetus exhibits a severe abnormality. The third view, the one held by Pro-Choice adherents, is that any decision regarding a possible abortion should be made by the pregnant woman after consultation with her doctor. This group maintains that the expectant mother has the exclusive right to decide what is best for her body.

All three of those views appear to have merit, so what must our nation do to resolve the dilemma surrounding abortion rights? Do not expect our country to resolve that huge argument about abortions, but I do believe changes in tactics by both sides, together with bipartisan actions by all concerned, could alleviate the problem considerably. The fundamental reason for the high number of abortions in our society is the widespread occurrences of unwanted pregnancies, especially among young single women. If we could only reduce the number of unwanted pregnancies, we could take a giant step forward in substantially reducing the abortion rate in America, but how can that be accomplished? Practical ways of reducing unwanted pregnancies and abortions are suggested in a later chapter of this book.

I must confess I have great difficulty in firming up my personal views regarding abortion rights. Many of you most likely share my concerns and questions as well. First, I am basically opposed to abortion, but I have never had a wife, daughter, granddaughter, sister, or other loved one who contemplated an abortion because of an unwanted pregnancy or other severe complications. I am not sure my stance toward abortion would remain the same if I did have a loved one in desperate circumstances facing such a life-changing decision. Until I walk in another person's shoes, how can I judge that person's responses to dire situations in their life? I firmly believe a woman has a fundamental and constitutional right to choose what is done to her body, but I have reservations if her decision affects an unborn fetus. I am still struggling with that concern.

It seems reasonable to me that an abortion should be allowed in the event of rape, incest, or endangerment of the woman's life. But, who decides what particular circumstance justifies an abortion? The religious right claims all abortion decisions should be made in the light of Scripture, but whose interpretation of the Bible should we follow? Must we rely on our own interpretation of the Bible, or that of our local church, or the President of the Southern Baptist Convention, or the Pope of the Catholic Church, or the head of Planned Parenthood, or the President of the United States of America, or the Supreme Court of our land, or some other distinguished individual or religious entity? In addition to the teaching of Scripture, we must consider the constitutional rights of both the expectant mother and the father of her unborn fetus. The abortion rights issue in America is a tough nut to crack, one we cannot resolve in our study, but we will consider it further in a subsequent chapter of this book.

Homosexual rights and gay marriage represent a second moral issue of major importance to social conservatives. The religious right perceives homosexuality as an acquired lifestyle rather than a result of genetics, and they consider any manner of homosexual relations to be a sin. The medical community has abundant data indicating genetics is a major factor in determining sexual orientation, but fundamentalist conservatives reject that data. America's gay population and many moderate Christians accept the argument of some in the medical profession that sexual orientation is determined to a great extent by genetics. It is also believed that family environment has a significant impact on sexual orientation. It is beyond the scope of our study to ascertain which side is right on the homosexual rights issue. Our task is to delineate the Biblical basis for the religious right's beliefs on that hot-button issue.

The Bible includes a number of passages dealing with homosexuality, and the religious right justifies their position by quoting those Scripture passages. Bible passages addressing homosexuality are found in both the Old Testament and the New Testament.

> The LORD said to Moses, "Speak to the Israelites and say to them: 'I am the LORD your God. You must not do as they do in Egypt, where you used to live, and you must not do as they do in the land of Caanan, where I am bringing you. Do not follow their practices. You must obey my laws and be careful to follow my decrees. I am the LORD your God.....Do not lie with a man as one lies with a woman; that is detestable.'"
> --Leviticus 18:1-4,22 NIV

> "If a man lies with a man as one lies with a woman, both of them have done what is detestable. They must be put to death; their blood will be on their own heads."
> --Leviticus 20:13 NIV

Moses was leading God's chosen people, Israel, from bondage in Egypt to a new life in the land of Caanan, the Promised Land. God gave Moses a code of laws to reveal His will with respect to the Israelites' conduct in Caanan.

We refer to that code of laws for Israel as the Mosaic Law. The Book of Leviticus is included in the Mosaic Law. Leviticus, chapter 18, presents God's instructions to His people concerning unlawful sexual relations. Verse 22 includes homosexual relations as one of those forbidden sexual activities. Leviticus, chapter 20, verse 13, spells out the prescribed punishment for homosexual relations.

Similar admonitions against homosexual activity are presented in the New Testament. Romans, chapter 1, proclaims God's wrath against sinful humankind, primarily Gentiles who did not have a close relationship with the Creator.

Therefore God gave them over in the sinful desires of their hearts to sexual impurity for the degrading of their bodies with one another. They exchanged the truth of God for a lie, and worshiped and served created things rather than the Creator---who is forever praised. Amen. Because of this, God gave them over to shameful lusts. Even their women exchanged natural relations for unnatural ones. In the same way the men also abandoned natural relations with women and were inflamed with lust for one another. Men committed indecent acts with other men, and received in themselves the due penalty for their perversion.....Although they know God's righteous decree that those who do such things deserve death, they not only continue to do these very things but also approve of those who practice them.
--Romans 1:24-27,32 NIV

Do you not know that the wicked will not inherit the kingdom of God? Do not be deceived: Neither the sexually immoral nor idolaters nor adulterers nor male prostitutes nor homosexual offenders nor thieves nor

the greedy nor drunkards nor slanderers nor swindlers will inherit the kingdom of God.
--1 Corinthians 6:9-10 NIV

The passage in Romans, chapter 1, warns of the results of Godless living. God gave sinful humankind over to all kinds of evil and wicked conduct, including homosexual relations among both men and women. Verse 32 includes those people who practice immoral and wicked living and others who approve of such conduct. The passage in the Book of 1 Corinthians includes homosexual offenders in the long list of wicked people who will not inherit the Kingdom of God. The precise meaning of "will not inherit the kingdom of God" in verse 9 is debatable, and interpretation of that phrase is left as an additional study exercise for the readers. I believe we can safely say, however, 1 Corinthians, chapter 6, does condemn homosexuality.

Fundamentalist Christians look at homosexuality as an acquired lifestyle, and as such it does not qualify for special consideration under the United States Constitution. The religious right refuses to categorize sexual orientation with race, gender, and age, which do receive discrimination protection under the Constitution. Gay marriage is an area of homosexual rights which has been most troublesome. Social conservatives do not recognize marriages of two individuals of the same sex, including any form of civil union which provides basic spousal benefits such as medical insurance, survivor pensions, and community property rights. Battles over gay marriage are being waged across our nation in state legislatures and in Congress, and the religious right is heavily involved in those struggles.

Social conservatives claim the Bible recognizes only marriage between a man and a woman. One verse of

Scripture in the creation account contained in the Book of Genesis clarifies their view on marriage.

> For this cause a man shall leave his father and his mother, and shall cleave to his wife; and they shall become one flesh.
> --Genesis 2:24 NAS

Marriage, or the home, was the first institution ordained by God, and that marriage was between one man and one woman, for the purpose of procreation. A multitude of Scripture passages throughout both the Old Testament and the New Testament affirm that initial definition of marriage. However, the Bible is silent with regard to any form of civil union, similar to marriage, between individuals of the same sex. Keep in mind the intent of this study is not to affirm or refute the views of social conservatives on the issues of homosexual rights and gay marriage. We are simply attempting to define their views on those issues.

Euthanasia is a sanctity of life issue of great concern to the religious right. They stand firmly against any form of "mercy killing" wherein a physician, hospital, spouse, family member, or other person assists a helpless and terminally ill individual end his or her life. We have witnessed numerous battles in which the religious right attempted to prevent parents, hospitals, or family members from "pulling the plug" on patients who were in a vegetable state with no chance of recovery. Quite often, terminally ill patients suffering intense pain, facing an extremely poor quality of life, and with no hope of improvement, prefer to just end it all. Unfortunately, many of those gravely ill folks are incapable of expressing their desires, except for those who make their wishes known in medical directives. Social conservatives view euthanasia in much the same light as abortion. They believe the Bible condemns euthanasia, and they work diligently to get laws passed making such mercy killings illegal. A significant number of moderate Christians disagree with the religious right. They believe it is inhumane to prolong the life of a terminally ill and suffering patient when their family and/or physicians determine the patient should be allowed to die peacefully and naturally.

Fundamentalist Christians also strive to include the teaching of creationism, or intelligent design, along with evolution in public school science classes. Evolution is an established scientific theory, supported by centuries of research and reams of reliable data. On the other hand, creationism, a fundamental Christian tenet, is a religious belief based solely on the Biblical account of creation in the Book of Genesis. The religious right's interpretation of the First Amendment to our Constitution permits teaching of Christian religious beliefs in public schools, hence they demand inclusion of creationism as a parallel scientific theory to evolution. Most moderate Christians reject mixing science and religion in public schools.

It is my opinion that the Scriptures address the "who" and "why" of creation, whereas science focuses on the "when" and "how." I am a devout Christian, and I believe strongly in the Biblical account of creation, but I do not believe science and the Bible are contradictory. I do not understand how it can be, but I am convinced science and Scripture are fully compatible. My view is that scientific facts, the works of God, are totally consistent with the Bible, the Word of God. Humankind does not yet possess the knowledge to ascertain one hundred percent correlation between the Bible and valid scientific findings, but I am confident it does exist.

State-sanctioned prayer in public schools is another hot-button issue among social conservatives. They maintain the First Amendment to our Constitution guarantees freedom of religious expression, in any place at any time, even in public schools. That interpretation essentially negates separation of church and state, a practice that has for the most part defined our nation's history. Students are now permitted to pray in public schools, but not in a school-directed format. A majority of moderate Christians oppose state-sponsored prayer in our public schools, simply because it would lead to the teaching of a particular religion or to favoring one religion over others. They interpret the First Amendment to mean freedom from religion as well as freedom of religion.

Allowing public school administrators or teachers to sponsor or dictate prayer in the classroom would surely raise all kinds of questions. For example, what kind of prayer would be allowed? Could it be a Catholic prayer, a Protestant prayer, a Jewish prayer, an Islam prayer, a Hindu prayer, or a prayer from some other religion? Social conservatives demand prayers of their choosing, namely Christian prayers, but all students do not come from a Christian religion. This is just another example of the religious right attempting to force their religious beliefs and practices on everyone. The big over-riding question is, "Who is responsible for teaching religion to our children?" Is the answer parents, churches, or our public schools? I believe the responsibility for teaching religion to our children should rest on parents, churches, and private religious schools, rather than on public schools. That view is not shared by the religious right, however, so they continue to press for state-sponsored prayer, specifically Christian prayer, in our public schools. The prayer in school issue is especially controversial because it involves both religion and constitutional concerns.

Another freedom of religion issue championed by the religious right is posting the Ten Commandments in government buildings and on government property. Traditionally, that particular religious expression has been allowed, with few complaints registered against such postings. The political climate has changed in recent years, however, and we hear more and more protests against posting the Ten Commandments in government facilities. This is a hot-button issue of great interest to social conservatives, but for the most part moderate Christians do not seem to care very much one way or the other. Objections to posting the Ten Commandments come primarily from extreme-left liberal Christians and from non-Christians. This is more of a constitutional issue, depending on one's interpretation of the First Amendment to our Constitution.

Closely related to abortion is embryonic stem cell research, another sanctity of life issue. Fundamentalist Christians object strongly to the use of embryos in stem cell research, even those embryos slated to be discarded, or destroyed, by fertility clinics. They claim an embryo is analogous to a fetus and thus should not be destroyed in stem cell research. The religious right seems to ignore the fact that a multitude of frozen embryos will ultimately be discarded anyway by fertility clinics, with absolutely no benefit to medical research. More moderate Christians, as well as a sizable number of social conservatives, believe those "doomed" embryos in fertility clinics are good candidates for use in stem cell research to find possible cures for severe spinal injuries and dread diseases such as Parkinson and cancer. I believe one could conceivably develop a sound Biblical argument against aborting a fetus in the womb of an expectant mother, but it seems to be quite a stretch to apply the same argument to the use of discarded frozen embryos in stem cell research.

All those religious, moral, and social issues championed by the religious right belong under the Republican Party's "family values" tent. The Christian Coalition and the Republican Party place utmost emphasis on those issues important to them, but they choose to ignore other social ills afflicting our country. They give only lip service to poverty in our society and around the world, millions of our nation's children without health insurance, rampant personal and corporate greed and corruption, the spread of AIDS and other diseases around the world, rapid degradation of our environment, high divorce rates within our society and the religious right, and the high incidence of marriage infidelity in America, even among social conservatives. The bottom line is that fundamentalist Christians focus on causes they deem to be religious and moral in nature, to the detriment of social causes considered to be more important by moderate Christians. It is simply a matter of priorities for our country, and subsequent chapters of this book are devoted to determining how Biblical teaching relates to those priorities.

We have attempted to define the overall agenda of the religious right, realizing that all social conservatives do not agree on each of the issues. There are, of course, other causes important to various segments of the Christian Coalition, but we have enumerated those issues which seem to be in the mainstream of social conservatives' political involvement.

Agenda of the Religious Right

Chapter 3

Priorities of Moderate Christians

Moderate Christians are not a well-organized, cohesive, and focused religious entity like the religious right. They harbor diverse views regarding religious, moral, and social issues dividing our country, and they are tolerant of people with conflicting beliefs. For example, numerous moderate Christians oppose abortion and gay marriage, but they do not share the consuming passion of social conservatives for those causes. Moderate Christians place a greater emphasis on ministry to the poor, the sick, the oppressed, and the downtrodden elements of our society.

A significant number of fundamentalist conservatives are single-issue voters. That is, they support political candidates who agree with them on those issues most important to social conservatives. That all-important concern is abortion rights for many in the religious right, but for others it is gay marriage, prayer in public schools, or some other religious or moral issue. On the other hand, moderate Christians are less likely to be single-issue voters. They are more interested in political candidates' stance on a broad range of issues rather than their position on one overriding concern. A sizable number of moderate Christians agree with the religious right on one or more religious or moral issues, but at the same time support political candidates who are opposed by the Christian Coalition.

It is difficult to characterize moderate Christians because of the diversity within their ranks. For purposes of this study, however, we consider moderate Christians to be those believers who place the highest priority on social ills afflicting our country, rather than on the religious and moral causes of the religious right. We must remember though that quite a few moderate Christians do indeed support social conservatives on one or more of their hot-button issues. We must also recognize that left-wing liberals and many citizens with no religious affiliation share the views of moderate Christians on a number of divisive religious, moral, and social concerns. Let us now define the overall priorities set forth by moderate Christians, noting we will surely encounter some inconsistencies as we do so.

We stated previously that both fundamentalist conservatives and moderate Christians consider evangelism to be their highest priority. Two Scripture passages state clearly the Biblical mandate to share the Gospel of Jesus Christ with all peoples of the world.

> Then Jesus came to them and said, "All authority in heaven and on earth has been given to me. Therefore go and make disciples of all nations, baptizing them in the name of the Father and of the Son and of the Holy

Spirit, and teaching them to obey everything I have commanded you. And surely I am with you always, to the very end of the age."
--Matthew 28:18-20 NIV

So when they met together, they asked him, "Lord, are you at this time going to restore the kingdom to Israel?" He said to them: "It is not for you to know the times or dates the Father has set by his own authority. But you will receive power when the Holy Spirit comes on you; and you will be my witnesses in Jerusalem, and in all Judea and Samaria, and to the ends of the earth."
--Acts 1:6-8 NIV

The passage in the Book of Matthew is sometimes referred to as the Great Commission. It commands all Christians to "make disciples" in all the nations of the world. The passage in the Book of Acts reiterates that command to share the Gospel, starting in our local communities and reaching throughout the world.

A key element of our overall witness to the world is the way we live our lives, our living witness. Both moderate Christians and social conservatives do a commendable job of reaching the world with their verbal witness. The manner in which we relate to people, including other Christians as well as non-Christians, is a good indicator of the effectiveness of our living witness. How we are perceived by those around us speaks volumes about our living witness. Our attitudes and actions toward other people are of prime importance, so that is a topic we will address at great length in subsequent chapters of this book.

The new Baptist alliance organized recently by former President Jimmy Carter, referred to herein as the New

Baptist Covenant, is representative of moderate Christians. We have all heard the slogan, "What would Jesus do?" The New Baptist Covenant interprets a Scripture passage in the Gospel of Luke as the answer to that question, defined as the "Jesus agenda."

> He went to Nazareth, where he had been brought up, and on the Sabbath day he went into the synagogue, as was his custom. And he stood up to read. The scroll of the prophet Isaiah was handed to him. Unrolling it, he found the place where it is written: "The Spirit of the Lord is on me, because he has anointed me to preach good news to the poor. He has sent me to proclaim freedom for the prisoners and recovery of sight for the blind, to release the oppressed, to proclaim the year of the Lord's favor." Then he rolled up the scroll, gave it back to the attendant and sat down. The eyes of everyone in the synagogue were fastened on him, and he began by saying to them, "Today this scripture is fulfilled in your hearing."
> --Luke 4:16-21 NIV

> The Spirit of the Sovereign LORD is on me, because the LORD has anointed me to preach good news to the poor. He has sent me to bind up the brokenhearted, to proclaim freedom for the captives and release from darkness for the prisoners, to proclaim the year of the LORD's favor and the day of vengeance of our God, to comfort all who mourn,
> --Isaiah 61:1-2 NIV

> At that very time Jesus cured many who had diseases, sickness and evil spirits, and gave sight to many who were blind. So he replied to the messengers, "Go back and report to John what you have seen and heard: The

blind receive sight, the lame walk, those who have leprosy are cured, the deaf hear, the dead are raised, and the good news is preached to the poor."
--Luke 7:21-22 NIV

Jesus frequently went into the synagogues on the Sabbath to read Old Testament Scriptures and interpret them for the people. In the passage from Luke, chapter 4, He quoted from the prophet Isaiah. The passage in Luke, chapter 7, is Jesus' response to messengers from John the Baptist when they asked Him if He was the Messiah promised in the Old Testament.

The passages from the Book of Luke summarize Jesus' understanding of His own mission. He was the fulfillment of prophecy by Isaiah and others many centuries earlier. Jesus' mission clearly included ministry to the physical needs of the poor, the sick, the blind, the oppressed, and the captives in the society of His day. As Christians, we are to emulate Jesus, our perfect example, so our mission is also to minister to the physical needs of the weak, sick, helpless, oppressed, and downtrodden in our society. We are to carry on the Jesus agenda. A spiritual message can certainly be gleaned from each phrase in the passages from the Book of Luke, but we dare not ignore the demand to meet the physical needs of those around us. That, I believe, is a fundamental responsibility of all Christians, regardless of our differences in theology, politics, and ideology.

Our society today is much more complex than that of the first century AD, but the Jesus agenda still applies. Extreme poverty exists in America and around the world, many of our citizens do not have access to adequate health care, control of dread diseases such as AIDS is grossly deficient, care for the very old and the very young is inadequate, equal educational opportunities are not available to everyone, many of our citizens lack suitable employment opportunities, all workers do not earn livable wages, our legal system favors wealthy and powerful elements in our society, we have an inequitable and unfair tax system, oppression of the weak and helpless in our midst is widespread, special-interest groups and greedy businesses abuse our environment, and greed and corruption permeate our society. All our nation's resources must be utilized if we really want to reduce the social ills afflicting America. A joint effort is required by individual citizens, families, churches, local and state governments, and our national government. An undertaking of such magnitude must involve politics, so the priorities of Christians, as well as our governments, are extremely important. Differences in theology, ideology, and politics must be set aside as we address the many social ills afflicting our country.

Moderate Christians champion a ministry of compassion and justice, as opposed to a ministry that divides and judges our people. Their goal is to decrease the emphasis on divisive issues such as theological differences, abortion rights, gay marriage, euthanasia, and prayer in public schools. Moderate Christians strive to pull all people of faith into a cooperative effort to reduce poverty and disease, to eliminate oppression and discrimination, to provide equal opportunities to all citizens, and to reduce greed and corruption in our society. That is a ministry of inclusion rather than one of division, and one which I believe follows the Jesus agenda.

In Jesus' day, the weak and helpless were orphans, widows, and aliens. Who are the weak and helpless in our society? The list must include families living in extreme poverty, with low incomes, who cannot afford decent housing, warm clothing, sufficient food, and adequate health care. Single-parent families constitute a sizable and increasing percentage of such families. Help for families in need is available through welfare systems, charities, Medicaid programs, churches, and individual giving, but more must be done. Ghetto and slum neighborhoods in most of our cities are home for the forgotten masses in America. Moderate Christians seek to improve the lives of those unfortunate citizens who cannot help themselves.

A multitude of senior citizens are counted in the weak and helpless of our society. A very large number of them live on fixed incomes insufficient to provide the basic necessities of life. Again, some help is available to them from various sources, but many of their dire needs remain unmet. Moderate Christians are sensitive to the needs of our older citizens, and they strive to improve their quality of life. As our nation ages, care for our older people will become a greater burden.

Young children also account for a significant number of the impoverished members of our society. A sizable percentage of the poor children in our society belong to immigrant families, both legal and illegal. The most pressing needs for those young children are nutritious meals and adequate health care. Help is also available for those unfortunate poor children, primarily through school nutrition programs, food stamps, other government programs, and private charities, but more help is needed. Moderate Christians are active in seeking ways to provide additional help for impoverished families with young children.

Other segments of our population are also weak and helpless. Our homeless population is large and growing, we have an increasing number of mentally and physically handicapped citizens, more and more of our senior adults require fulltime care in either nursing facilities or with their families, we have a significant population of fatherless and motherless young children, the incidence of dread diseases such as AIDS and cancer remains high, our prisons are full of untreated victims of substance abuse, and we have a rapidly growing population of military veterans with severe physical injuries or emotional problems. All those needs are crying out to be met, and moderate Christians strive to provide relief in each area. However, the problems are of such magnitude that their resolution demands resources that can be provided only by state and federal governments.

The poor, weak, and helpless in our society do not have equal legal representation, which is a form of oppression. A vast majority of our incarcerated citizens come from poor families and low-income neighborhoods, and a disproportionate number of them come from minority segments of our population. Those poor prison inmates usually serve much longer sentences than do their middle-class and wealthy cell mates who commit the same crimes. The death row population in our prisons is made up almost exclusively of poor inmates. Well-to-do criminals seldom get the death penalty. Huge numbers of our poorer citizens are serving prison time for relatively minor offences, whereas few wealthier individuals are convicted for the same offences.

Why do we have such an imbalance in our criminal justice system? The answer of course is money. People with wealth have connections and access to well-qualified and capable attorneys. On the other hand, poor defendants are usually represented by court-appointed attorneys who are quite often lazy or incompetent, or they do not have the time required to adequately defend their clients. As a result, poor defendants are convicted at a much higher rate than their wealthier counterparts, and they are given significantly longer prison sentences. On top of that, poor inmates do not have the financial wherewithal to pursue appeals, which is especially important in cases of wrongful conviction. The answer to this dilemma is to level the playing field. That means more money must be committed to provide adequate legal representation for all citizens. The Republican Party has historically opposed such expenditures of government funds, and the religious right is an integral part of the Republican Party.

Poor and uneducated citizens in other segments of our society are penalized as well, simply because they cannot afford competent legal counsel. Those unfortunate folks are short-changed on insurance claims, in real estate transactions, in property foreclosures, by high loan shark interest rates, and in civil litigations of all kinds. Those people who can least afford it wind up paying more for all types of insurance, credit card interest rates, mortgage interest rates, and various other time-pay transactions. Moderate Christians are concerned about this widespread legal oppression of our poorest citizens, and they seek to eliminate some of the biases and inequalities in our justice system.

Education is extremely important in our high-tech modern economy, but higher education is increasingly more expensive. Middle class families find it difficult to pay for their children's college educations, and it is virtually impossible for poor families to fund higher education for their children. Scholarships, grants, and student loans are available for some low-income families, but a majority of our children living in poverty do not obtain college degrees. As a result, those children are stuck with low-paying jobs, and our struggling poor class of citizens is perpetuated. Moderate Christians are sympathetic to the education needs of our poorer population, and they strive to make higher education attainable for all citizens in our country. The financial burden is great, but America must not allow so many of our young people to miss out on college educations.

Unequal education opportunities lead to unequal employment opportunities. The demand for low-skill laborers is diminishing in our high-tech world, so our nation must do something to equip low-skill workers for high-tech jobs. Other than colleges and trade schools, the logical way to do that is with job training programs. That is an expensive undertaking, but it is something our country must do if we are to remain competitive with other countries around the world. Workers must also be able to earn livable wages on their jobs. Otherwise, the ranks of those living in poverty would increase, and our nation's overall standard of living would go down. Moderate Christians are pressing for equal employment opportunities for all of our people and livable wages for all workers.

Moderate Christians are becoming more and more concerned about environmental pollution. Mining companies, the oil industry, petrochemical plants, manufacturing companies, factories, and land developers have no qualms about damaging our environment. They are more concerned about bottom-line profits than the effects of their operations on the environment. Those businesses spew pollutants into the atmosphere, poisoning the air we breathe, and discharge poisonous chemicals into lakes, rivers, and streams, thus polluting the water we drink. Our land is poisoned by greedy corporations and businesses; they destroy or alter wildlife sanctuaries, they deface our pristine parks and forests, and they cause flooding and fire control problems around our cities.

We have heard an ongoing debate about global warming over the last twenty or so years. Claims and counterclaims go back and forth about the reality and causes of global warming, especially with regard to human-generated gasses. Recent and reliable studies indicate that industrial pollution, together with the pollution produced by the automobiles and trucks we drive, account for a significant portion of the global warming experienced by the world over the last few decades. The Bible speaks clearly about our environment.

> Then God said, "Let Us make man in Our image, according to our likeness; and let them rule over the fish of the sea and over the birds of the sky and over the cattle and over all the earth, and over every creeping thing that creeps on the earth." And God created man in His own image, in the image of God He created him; male and female He created them. And God blessed them; and God said to them, "Be fruitful and multiply, and fill the earth, and subdue it; and rule over the fish of the sea and over the birds of the sky, and over every living thing that moves on the earth." Then God said, "Behold, I have given you every plant yielding seed that is on the surface of the earth, and every tree which has fruit yielding seed; it shall be food for you; and to every beast of the earth and to every bird of the sky and to every thing that moves on the earth which has life, I have given every green plant for food"; and it was so.
> --Genesis 1:26-30 NAS

> And God blessed Noah and his sons and said to them, "Be fruitful and multiply, and fill the earth. "And the fear of you and the terror of you shall be on every beast of the earth and on every bird of the sky; with everything that creeps on the ground, and all the fish of the sea, into your hand they are given. "Every moving thing that is alive shall be food for you; I give all to you, as I gave the green plant."
> --Genesis 9:1-3 NAS

The passage in the Book of Genesis, chapter 1, concludes the Biblical account of creation. God created first the heavens and the earth on which we live, including the universe with its suns, moons, stars, and other heavenly bodies. Next, God separated the earth into dry land and seas. He then added all kinds of vegetation, creatures of the sea, winged creatures of the air, and animal life on the ground. God completed His six-day creation work with the creation of humankind, represented by Adam and Eve. God gave humankind dominion over all of His creation, meaning humans are responsible for preserving, maintaining, and taking care of the earth and all of its creatures and resources. Humankind's dominion over all the earth was reiterated by God to Noah after the great flood.

As God's caretaker of His creation, humans are to nurture and cultivate all plant life, using it for the benefit of both themselves and other creatures of the earth. Humankind is also responsible for protecting and taking care of all creatures of the sea, air, and land.

> And the LORD God planted a garden toward the east, in Eden; and there He placed the man whom He had formed.....Then the LORD God took the man and put him into the garden of Eden to cultivate it and keep it.
> --Genesis 2:8,15 NAS

> Now the man had relations with his wife Eve, and she conceived and gave birth to Cain, and she said, "I have gotten a manchild with the help of the LORD." And again, she gave birth to his brother Abel. And Abel was a keeper of the flocks, but Cain was a tiller of the ground.
> --Genesis 4:1-2 NAS

God placed Adam in the lush, beautiful, and productive Garden of Eden and instructed him to cultivate it and take care of it. Life for the "first family" of Adam and Eve was very simple. Their first son, Cain, was a farmer, and their second son, Abel, was a herdsman. Those first human beings subdued and gained control of the creatures in their midst, and they had all the earth's resources at their disposal. God allows humankind to employ all creatures of the earth, but not to exploit them and abuse them. Humans can develop and utilize the earth's resources for their benefit, but not waste them and destroy them.

Our society today is much more complex than that of those ancient human beings, but Biblical guidelines still apply. We can harness the earth's many resources, develop them, and use them for the benefit of both humankind and other creatures of the earth. However, we must preserve the earth's natural beauty. We dare not waste its resources, and we must not pollute our water, air, or land. God also gives us dominion over all creatures of the earth. We can subdue them and use them for our benefit, but we must not exploit them or destroy them maliciously. It is our responsibility to care for and protect the creatures of the earth. Moderate Christians are sensitive to Biblical teaching pertaining to the environment, and they support individual practices and government policies which protect and preserve the earth's resources and creatures of the water, air, and land.

We have noted that moderate Christians have diverse views with regard to controversial religious, moral, and social issues in our society, so it has been difficult to characterize them. They are less uniform than their counterparts, the religious right, in their beliefs about abortion rights, gay marriage, prayer in public schools, using embryos in stem cell research, children's health insurance, government aid for the poor and helpless, affirmative action programs, equal opportunities for all citizens, environmental issues, and other controversial concerns in today's society. We have based our definition of moderate Christians on one overriding factor. They place a higher priority on the multitude of social ills afflicting our nation than they do on those controversial religious and moral causes championed by the religious right.

Chapter 4

What God Expected of His Chosen People

We have defined the mainstream agenda of the religious right and discussed priorities of more moderate Christians. Social conservatives cling to strong and somewhat narrow-minded beliefs about controversial religious, moral, and social issues. They oppose abortion, euthanasia, homosexuality, gay marriage, and use of embryos in stem cell research, and they push for state-sanctioned prayer in public schools, posting the Ten Commandments in public facilities, and teaching creationism in public school science classes. The religious right is passionate about those causes, and they are active in the political arena to promote their agenda and get their beliefs incorporated into our laws and government policies. Fundamentalist Christians claim the Bible supports their views on the issues, and they are intolerant of those with different beliefs.

Moderate Christians are a more loosely defined religious entity, and they are more tolerant of people who disagree with them on religious, moral, and social issues. Actually, quite a few moderate Christians concur with the beliefs of the religious right on a number of controversial issues, but they are not as fervent and not as active as social conservatives regarding those causes. Moderate Christians place a greater emphasis on addressing the social ills afflicting our country. They are deeply concerned about widespread poverty in America and around the world, unchecked dread diseases such as AIDS, oppression of the weak and helpless in our society, lack of adequate health care for all our citizens, unequal education and employment opportunities, lack of legal representation for poor people, degradation and abuse of our environment, greed and corruption in our society, and other similar social ills. Moderate Christians emphasize a ministry of compassion and justice, rather than an agenda that divides and judges people, and they also claim the Bible supports their priorities.

Can the overall Christian community, and our nation as a whole, best please God by adhering to the social conservative agenda of the religious right, or should we adopt the broader social ministry of moderate Christians? Choosing one does not necessarily mean the other is wrong. It simply means one is more in concert than the other with the overall teaching of Scripture. Let us first determine what God expected of His people, the Jews, in the Old Testament, and then what He desires of His people, the Church, in the New Testament. We will then be better equipped to determine what God expects of His people today.

God's chosen people in the Old Testament were the children of Israel, or the nation Israel, often referred to as God's covenant people. Abraham, or Abram, is considered the Father of Israel, and God's call of Abraham to that role is presented in the Book of Genesis in the Bible. God established a covenant with Abraham, and later with his son, Isaac, and his grandson, Jacob, to raise up a great nation from Abraham's descendants. God promised to give them the land of Canaan, the Promised Land, a land of milk and honey. Because of a great famine in Canaan, Jacob (or Israel) and his twelve sons and their families relocated to Egypt. Eventually, the Israelites were enslaved by the Pharaoh in Egypt for some four hundred years, and Abraham's descendants numbered over 600,000 men, plus women and children, at the end the four hundred years.

God called Moses, an Israelite, to lead His chosen people out of bondage in Egypt, back to the land of Canaan, their Promised Land. That exodus from Egypt to Canaan consumed forty years, during which time God gave Moses a code of laws to reveal His will with respect to the Israelites' conduct in Canaan. We refer to that code of laws for Israel as the Mosaic Law, which includes the Ten Commandments. Occasionally, reference to the Law means only the Ten Commandments, but generally it includes all the divinely instituted commands and precepts mediated through Moses to govern the overall conduct of God's people. The entire Mosaic Law is included in the first five books of the Old Testament, from Genesis to Deuteronomy. Detailed instructions are given with regard to worship practices, sacrifices and offerings, special feasts, observance of the Sabbath, dietary restrictions, family responsibilities, tithing, financial responsibilities, sexual considerations, laws and courts, punishment for sin, and every other aspect of conduct.

Obviously, such a demanding and complex set of rules and regulations is virtually impossible to follow, so what did God really expect of His people? The remaining books in the Old Testament show us how God dealt with His people

Israel. We see a repetitive cycle of Israel turning from one true God to pagan gods, their practicing a lifestyle of sin and immorality, God's disciplining and judgment of Israel for their sins, the people's repentance for their sins, and God's forgiveness and restoration of the Israelites to their status as God's people. What exactly were the sins of Israel that brought on God's judgment? The historical and prophetic books of the Old Testament, from Joshua through Malachi, cover a multitude of sins and wrongdoings committed by the people of Israel, but I believe we can condense them into three categories.

It is worthwhile for us to review the Ten Commandments, however, before we consider those three sin categories. Those basic commandments are the foundation for all the detailed instructions and precepts incorporated into the overall Mosaic Law, as well as a code of conduct for people today.

> And God spoke all these words: "I am the LORD your God, who brought you out of Egypt, out of the land of slavery. "You shall have no other gods before me. "You shall not make yourself an idol in the form of anything in heaven above or on the earth beneath or in the waters below. You shall not bow down to them or worship them; for I, the LORD your God, am a jealous God, punishing the children for the sin of the fathers to the third and fourth generation of those who hate me, but showing love to a thousand generations of those who love me and keep my commandments. "You shall not misuse the name of the LORD your God, for the LORD will not hold anyone guiltless who misuses his name. "Remember the Sabbath day by keeping it holy. Six days you shall labor and do all your work, but the seventh day is a Sabbath to the LORD your God. On it you shall not do any work, neither you, nor your son or

daughter, nor your manservant or maidservant, nor your animals, nor the alien within your gates. For in six days the LORD made the heavens and the earth, the sea, and all that is in them, but he rested on the seventh day. Therefore the LORD blessed the Sabbath day and made it holy. "Honor your father and your mother, so that you may live long in the land the LORD your God is giving you. "You shall not murder. "You shall not commit adultery. "You shall not steal. "You shall not give false testimony against your neighbor. "You shall not covet your neighbor's house. You shall not covet your neighbor's wife, or his manservant or maidservant, his ox or donkey, or anything that belongs to your neighbor."
--Exodus 20:1-17 NIV

The first four commandments deal with the Israelites', and our, relationship with God, and they are of utmost importance. We cannot hope to obey the remaining commandments if we do not have a right relationship with the Lord. The last six commandments focus on our relationships with others, starting with our fathers and mothers. So, let us not forget that the sins of the Israelites, as well as our sins, are the result of either a wrong relationship with God or wrong relationships with one another.

The most significant and the most prevalent sin committed by the people of Israel was that of turning away from God and His ways and turning to false pagan gods. Israel's turning away from the Lord, and thus disobedience of His laws and precepts, is the main theme of the prophets' messages to the people of Israel. The primary responsibility of the prophets was to deliver God's messages to His people, but quite often those messages were not what the people wanted to hear. The Book of Judges contains numerous accounts of the Israelites turning from the Lord to pagan deities, God's judgment on them, their repentance, and God's deliverance and restoration.

> The Israelites did evil in the sight of the LORD; they forgot the LORD their God and served the Baals and the Asherahs. The anger of the LORD burned against Israel so that he sold them into the hands of Cushan-Rishathaim king of Aram Naharaim, to whom the Israelites were subject for eight years. But when they cried out to the LORD, he raised up for them a deliverer, Othniel son of Kenaz, Caleb's younger brother, who saved them. The spirit of the LORD came upon him, so that he became Israel's judge and went to war. The LORD gave Cushan-Rishathaim king of Aram into the hands of Othniel, who overpowered him. So the land had peace for forty years, until Othniel son of Kenaz died.
> --Judges 3:7-11 NIV

> Once again the Israelites did evil in the eyes of the LORD, and because they did this evil the LORD gave Eglon king of Moab power over Israel. Getting the Ammonites and Amalekites to join him, Eglon came and attacked Israel, and they took possession of the City of Palms. The Israelites were subject to Eglon king of Moab for eighteen years. Again the Israelites cried out to the LORD, and he gave them a deliverer--- Ehud, a left-handed man, the son of Gera the Benjamite. The Israelites sent him with tribute to Eglon king of Moab...."Follow me," he ordered, "for the LORD has given Moab, your enemy, into your hands." So they followed him down and, taking possession of the fords of the Jordan that led to Moab, they allowed no one to cross over. At that time they

struck down about ten thousand Moabites, all vigorous and strong; not a man escaped. That day Moab was made subject to Israel, and the land had peace for eighty years.
--Judges 3:12-15,28-30 NIV

These two episodes in Israel's history are typical examples of how God, or the Lord, dealt with His people. The Israelites would enjoy a period of peace and prosperity, but they would turn away from God and start serving pagan gods in their midst. The Lord would then allow a pagan nation to conquer Israel, and they would be under the dominion of that pagan nation for a number of years. The people would finally repent and cry out to the Lord, and He would raise up a deliverer to lead them out of bondage. Israel would have peace and prosperity for another long time period, and the cycle would be repeated.

The prophetic books of the Old Testament include similar accounts of Israel, or Judah, turning away from the Lord and turning to the worship of pagan gods or idols. Some of the prophets lived during the time when the twelve tribes of Israel were joined as the United Kingdom of Israel, whereas others lived after the twelve tribes of Israel were split into the Divided Kingdoms of Israel and Judah.

I will pronounce my judgments on my people because of their wickedness in forsaking me, in burning incense to other gods and in worshiping what their hands have made.
--Jeremiah 1:16 NIV

Hear the word of the LORD, O house of Jacob, all you clans of the house of Israel. This is what the LORD says: "What fault did your fathers find in me, that they strayed so far from me? They followed worthless idols

and became worthless themselves. They did not ask, 'Where is the LORD, who brought us up out of Egypt and led us through the barren wilderness, through a land of deserts and rifts, a land of drought and darkness, a land where no one travels and no one lives?' I brought you into a fertile land to eat its fruit and rich produce. But you came and defiled my land and made my inheritance detestable. The priests did not ask, 'Where is the LORD?' Those who deal with the law did not know me; the leaders rebelled against me. The prophets prophesied by Baal, following worthless idols."
--Jeremiah 2:4-8 NIV

These passages in the Book of Jeremiah give an account of Israel's long history of unfaithfulness. The Israelites repeatedly strayed from the Lord, the One who delivered them from bondage in Egypt and to the Promised Land of Canaan. The religious leaders and experts in the Law rebelled against God to serve pagan gods and idols. Through Jeremiah, the Lord pleaded with His people to return to Him, and He offered forgiveness and restoration if they would only repent.

Ezekiel, a prophet in Judah, delivered messages declaring God's judgment on the nation of Judah and its capital city, Jerusalem. His messages from the Lord came in the form of visions, and they came before the fall of Jerusalem to the Babylonians. One such vision came to Ezekiel when he was at his home, and it came in the presence of some elders (leaders of Judah). Ezekiel was in exile in Babylonia at the time of that vision.

In the sixth year, in the sixth month on the fifth day, while I was sitting in my house and the elders of Judah

were sitting before me, the hand of the Sovereign
LORD came upon me there.
--Ezekiel 8:1 NIV

Then he said to me, "Son of man, look toward the
north." So I looked, and in the entrance north of the
gate of the altar I saw this idol of jealousy. And he
said to me, "Son of man, do you see what they are
doing---the utterly detestable things the house of Israel
is doing here, things that will drive me far from my
sanctuary? But you will see things that are even more
detestable."
--Ezekiel 8:5-6 NIV

And he said to me, "Go in and see the wicked and
detestable things they are doing here." So I went in
and looked, and I saw portrayed all over the walls all
kinds of crawling things and detestable animals and all
the idols of the house of Israel. In front of them stood
seventy elders of the house of Israel, and Jaazaniah son
of Shaphan was standing among them. Each had a
censer in his hand, and a fragrant cloud of incense was
rising. He said to me, "Son of man, have you seen
what the elders of the house of Israel are doing in the
darkness, each at the shrine of his own idol? They say,
'The LORD does not see us; the LORD has forsaken the
land.'" Again, he said, "You will see them doing
things that are even more detestable."
--Ezekiel 8:9-13 NIV

Then he brought me to the entrance to the north gate of
the house of the LORD, and I saw women sitting there,
mourning for Tammuz. He said to me, "Do you see
this, son of man? You will see things that are even
more detestable than this."

--Ezekiel 8:14-15 NIV

He then brought me into the inner court of the house of the LORD, and there at the entrance to the temple, between the portico and the altar, were about twenty-five men. With their backs toward the temple of the LORD and their faces toward the east, they were bowing down to the sun in the east. He said to me, "Have you seen this, son of man? Is it a trivial matter for the house of Judah to do the detestable things they are doing here? Must they also fill the land with violence and continually provoke me to anger? Look at them putting the branch to their nose! Therefore I will deal with them in anger; I will not look on them with pity or spare them. Although they shout in my ears, I will not listen to them."
--Ezekiel 8:16-18 NIV

Ezekiel gave the exact time and place of this vision. He was at home while in exile in Babylonia when leaders from the other Judah exiles came to visit him. This particular vision focuses on the abhorrent worship practices in the temple back in Jerusalem. Verses 5-6 describe worship of a pagan god, the "idol of jealousy," inside the temple at the altar gate. That idol located near the altar provoked the Lord to jealousy; He did not want His people to be drawn to any other god. This form of jealousy is considered to be a positive attribute. Verses 9-13 depict animal worship inside the temple. The elders were burning incense and worshiping images of animals painted on the walls of a hidden area in the temple. The elders knew such worship of animals was forbidden by the Lord, but they believed He could not see them. Verses 14-15 portray women in the temple worshiping Tammuz, a Babylonian fertility god. By worshiping that pagan fertility god, the women were expressing their belief that Tammuz, rather than the Lord, would bring fertility to their land. We see in verses 16-18 sun worship in the temple, probably by priests. Sun worship was a common practice in the ancient pagan world, but the Israelites were forbidden to worship any thing or anyone other than their true God.

There are many other accounts in the Old Testament of the Israelites turning from Jehovah God to the pagan deities in their midst. Turning from the Lord to pagan deities did not necessarily mean the Israelites had stopped worshiping Jehovah God. Quite often, they worshiped both the Lord and pagan gods, so they still considered themselves to be God's people. They did not realize, however, that they could not do both; God demands His people's total allegiance. Their shared worship of the Lord, along with pagan deities, was superficial and insincere, and it was totally unacceptable to the Lord.

The Israelites' turning away from the Lord to pagan gods led to the second major category of sin, that of immorality and wicked living. The people of Israel took on the lifestyles and cultures of the pagan societies whose gods they worshiped. They were guilty of adultery, murder, cheating, lying, and all kinds of wickedness. The prophet Hosea's marriage to his unfaithful wife, Gomer, symbolized the relationship between the Lord and His unfaithful people, Israel. Gomer's marriage infidelity was analogous to Israel's spiritual infidelity.

Hear the word of the LORD, you Israelites, because the LORD has a charge to bring against you who live in the land: "There is no faithfulness, no love, no acknowledgment of God in the land. There is only cursing, lying and murder, stealing and adultery; they break all bounds, and bloodshed follows bloodshed. Because of this the land mourns, and all who live in it

waste away; the beasts of the field and the birds of the air and the fish of the sea are dying."
--Hosea 4:1-3 NIV

Through Hosea, the Lord charged Israel with turning away from Him, and He charged them with all kinds of sinful living. Verse 2 portrays Israel as a nation characterized by a complete breakdown of morality. Even nature was affected by the sins of the people. The land, the animals, the birds, and the fish were adversely affected by Israel's sins.

"You stumble day and night, and the prophets stumble with you. So I will destroy your mother---my people are destroyed from lack of knowledge. "Because you have rejected knowledge, I also reject you as my priests; because you have ignored the law of your God, I also will ignore your children. The more the priests increased, the more they sinned against me; they exchanged their Glory for something disgraceful. They feed on the sins of my people and relish their wickedness. And it will be: Like people, like priests. I will punish both of them for their ways and repay them for their deeds."
--Hosea 4:5-9 NIV

The priests were responsible for instructing the people in matters of the Law, but they failed to do so. The priests were just as guilty as the people, so God's judgment would come down on both the people and the religious leaders.

Another vision by the prophet Ezekiel indicates the wide range of sins committed by the Israelites in Jerusalem. Those detestable sins by the people were the result of their turning from God to the pagan deities all around them.

The word of the LORD came to me: "Son of man, will you judge her? Will you judge this city of bloodshed? Then confront her with all her detestable practices and say: 'This is what the Sovereign LORD says: O city that brings on herself doom by shedding blood in her midst and defiles herself by making idols, you have become guilty because of the blood you have shed and have become defiled by the idols you have made. You have brought your days to a close, and the end of your years has come. Therefore I will make you an object of scorn to the nations and a laughingstock to all the countries.....'"See how each of the princes of Israel who are in you uses his power to shed blood. In you they have treated father and mother with contempt; in you they have oppressed the alien and mistreated the fatherless and the widow. You have despised my holy things and desecrated my Sabbaths. In you are slanderous men bent on shedding blood; in you are those who eat at the mountain shrines and commit lewd acts. In you are those who dishonor their father's bed; in you are those who violate women during their period, when they are ceremonially unclean. In you one man commits a detestable offense with his neighbor's wife, another shamefully defiles his daughter-in-law, and another violates his sister, his own father's daughter. In you men accept bribes to shed blood; you take usury and excessive interest and make unjust gain from your neighbors by extortion. And you have forgotten me, declares the Sovereign LORD.'"
--Ezekiel 22:1-4,6-12 NIV

The inhabitants of Jerusalem worshiped idols in pagan shrines, shed innocent blood, treated their parents with contempt, committed all kinds of immoral sexual acts, did not observe the Sabbath, cheated their neighbors, and forgot the Lord. The preceding passage in Ezekiel is only one of numerous times the Bible addresses the sins of Israel and Judah.

> The LORD saw how great man's wickedness on the earth had become, and that every inclination of the thoughts of his heart was only evil all the time. The LORD was grieved that he had made man on the earth, and his heart was filled with pain. So the LORD said, "I will wipe mankind, whom I have created, from the face of the earth---men and animals, the creatures that move along the ground, and birds of the air---for I am grieved that I made them." But Noah found favor in the eyes of the LORD.....Now the earth was corrupt in God's sight and was full of violence. God saw how corrupt the earth had become, for all the people on earth had corrupted their ways. So God said to Noah, "I am going to put an end to all people, for the earth is filled with violence because of them. I am surely going to destroy both them and the earth."
> --Genesis 6:5-8,11-13 NIV

> But your inequities have separated you from your God; your sins have hidden his face from you, so that he will not hear. For your hands are stained with blood, your fingers with guilt. Your lips have spoken lies, and your tongue mutters wicked things. No one calls for justice; no one pleads his case with integrity. They rely on empty arguments and speak lies; they conceive trouble and give birth to evil.....Their deeds are evil deeds, and acts of violence are in their hands. Their feet rush into sin; they are swift to shed innocent blood. Their thoughts are evil thoughts; ruin and destruction mark their ways. The way of peace they do

not know; there is no justice in their paths. They have turned them into crooked roads; no one who walks in them will know peace.
--Isaiah 59:2-4,6b-8 NIV

From the time of Noah, when the Lord sent a great flood on the earth, people have lived sinful and corrupt lives. The historical books of the Bible and the prophets paint the picture of a rebellious people who turn from the one true God to worship false gods. They commit detestable sins of all kinds, including sins of immorality. God demands total allegiance from His people, and He hates sin, so such corrupt and sinful conduct brings on God's judgment.

The third major category of sin committed by the Israelites involved their treatment of the poor, weak, and helpless in their society. Mistreatment of the downtrodden is addressed by the prophets in numerous Scripture passages. Those sins against the poor and powerless include a legal system partial to the wealthy, oppression of the weak and helpless, defrauding poor people out of their homes and inheritances, bribery and extortion, dishonesty in the marketplace, cheating employees out of their wages, forcing people into slavery, and false teaching by the religious leaders. Throughout the Bible, God is a champion of those who cannot help themselves, and the Scriptures come down hard on those who abuse, neglect, or mistreat the poor and helpless among us.

The Mosaic Law defines in great detail how the Israelites were to treat one another, and the prophets charged the people of Israel with violating those laws and precepts. Let us consider just a few of the many Scripture passages addressing that critical aspect of the Israelites' conduct.

"For the LORD your God is the God of gods and the LORD of lords, the great, the mighty, and the awesome

God who does not show partiality, nor take a bribe.
"He executes justice for the orphan and the widow, and
shows His love for the alien by giving him food and
clothing.
--Deuteronomy 10:17-18 (NAS)

Learn to do right!   Seek justice, encourage the
oppressed. Defend the cause of the fatherless, plead
the case of the widow.
--Isaiah 1:17 NIV

"Do not pervert justice; do not show partiality to the
poor or favoritism to the great, but judge your neighbor
fairly."
--Leviticus 19:15 NIV

The LORD works righteousness and justice for all the
oppressed. He made known his ways to Moses, his
deeds to the people of Israel:....
--Psalm 103:6-7 NIV

"Because of the oppression of the weak and the
groaning of the needy, I will now arise," says the
LORD. "I will protect them from those who malign
them."
--Psalm 12:5 NIV

Selfishness and self-centeredness have characterized the
human race since the first sin of Adam and Eve in the
Garden of Eden. All human beings are born with a nature
and an environment inclined to sin; all of us have sinned.
The wealthy and strong have oppressed and mistreated the
poor and weak throughout the history of humankind. The
Scripture passages in Deuteronomy, Isaiah, Leviticus, and
Psalms inform us that such behavior is in violation of God's

laws and instructions to the people of Israel, and to us as well.

Prophets from Isaiah and Joel to Malachi charged the people of Israel and Judah with disobedience and perversion of God's commandments and precepts. They called for repentance by the people and proclaimed His judgment on those who did not turn back to the Lord and His ways.

Woe to those who make unjust laws, to those who issue oppressive decrees, to deprive the poor of their rights and withhold justice from the oppressed of my people, making widows their prey and robbing the fatherless.
--Isaiah 10:1-2 NIV

The oracle that Habakkuk the prophet received. How long, O LORD, must I call for help, but you do not listen? Or cry out to you, "Violence!" but you do not save? Why do you make me look at injustice? Why do you tolerate wrong? Destruction and violence are before me; there is strife, and conflict abounds. Therefore the law is paralyzed, and justice never prevails. The wicked hem in the righteous, so that justice is perverted.
--Habakkuk 1:1-4 NIV

Woe to those who plan inequity, to those who plot evil on their beds! At morning's light they carry it out because it is in their power to do it. They covet fields and seize them, and houses, and take them. They defraud a man of his home, a fellowman of his inheritance.
--Micah 2:1-2 NIV

> You hate the one who reproves in court and despise him who tells the truth. You trample on the poor and force him to give you grain. Therefore, though you have built stone mansions, you will not live in them; though you have planted lush vineyards, you will not drink their wine. For I know how many are your offenses and how great your sins. You oppress the righteous and take bribes and you deprive the poor of justice in the courts.
> --Amos 5:10-12 NIV

These Scripture passages are addressed primarily to those who pervert the law and the courts to cheat and oppress the poor and helpless. The charges enumerated are against the rulers, religious leaders, judges, and other powerful and wealthy people. Widows, orphans, and aliens represented needy and helpless people in Biblical times. They could not own property, and they had very little means of support. The poor and weak were those people who owned very limited material possessions, barely eked out a living, and were unable to defend themselves in the legal system. They were at the mercy of the rulers, judges, wealthy people, and religious leaders.

Those in power in Israel and Judah were guilty of establishing unjust laws and decrees, laws that would benefit themselves and penalize the poor and helpless in their society. The powerful and well connected plotted to cheat poor people out of their fields, homes, and inheritances. That was accomplished in a legal system wherein untruthful testimony was heard and tolerated, unjust laws were enforced, and judges were bribed. Extortion was utilized to obtain the meager possessions of poor people, and violence was quite often employed by those in power. The widows, orphans, and other helpless people were denied any means of help and support. The rulers, judges, and wealthy people used the spoils of unlawful and dishonest activities to maintain their high standard of living.

The people of Israel and Judah practiced slavery. Oftentimes, a person became a slave when he or she was captured in warfare; the victor in war took those who were conquered as slaves. Poor Israelites also became slaves as payment for debts they could not repay, and poor families even sold their children into slavery as payment of debts they owed.

> This is what the LORD says: "For three sins of Israel, even for four, I will not turn back my wrath. They sell the righteous for silver, and the needy for a pair of sandals. They trample on the heads of the poor as upon the dust of the ground and deny justice to the oppressed. Father and son use the same girl and so profane my holy name. They lie down beside every altar on garments taken in pledge. In the house of their god they drink wine taken as fines."
> --Amos 2:6-8 NIV

> Hear this, you who trample the needy and do away with the poor of the land, saying, "When will the New Moon be over that we may sell grain, and the Sabbath be ended that we may market wheat?"---skimping the measure, boosting the price and cheating with dishonest scales, buying the poor with silver and the needy for a pair of sandals, selling even the sweepings with the wheat.
> --Amos 8:4-6 NIV

People were sometimes sold into slavery for money (silver), and they were sold at other times for property, symbolized by a "pair of sandals." Wealthy people profaned the house of the Lord by drinking wine there after it had been taken as fines from poor people and by lying at the altar on garments of clothing taken as pledges for debts owed. Those debts were unjust and illegal, the result of false judgments and injustices against the poor and needy. Note also in the Book of Amos, chapter 2, verse 7, that father and son had sexual relations with the same girl, most likely a reference to a household servant. That is just one other way of abusing and taking advantage of a poor and helpless person.

Those in power used force and violence to take the possessions of others who were poor, needy, and powerless. The Bible presents few details regarding the nature of that violence, but it involved bloodshed, and most likely taking people's lives. Two things are clear, however; the shedding of blood was unjustified, and it was widespread.

"Woe to him who builds his palace by unrighteousness, his upper rooms by injustice, making his countrymen work for nothing, not paying them for their labor."...."But your eyes and your heart are set only on dishonest gain, on shedding innocent blood and on oppression and extortion."
--Jeremiah 22:13,17 NIV

The godly have been swept from the land; not one upright man remains. All men lie in wait to shed blood; each hunts his brother with a net. Both hands are skilled in doing evil; the ruler demands gifts, the judge accepts bribes, the powerful dictate what they desire---they all conspire together.
--Micah 7:2-3 NIV

The word of the LORD came to me: "Son of man, will you judge her? Will you judge this city of bloodshed? Then confront her with all her detestable practices...."'See how each of the princes of Israel

who are in you uses his power to shed blood. In you
they have treated father and mother with contempt; in
you they have oppressed the alien and mistreated the
fatherless and widow.'"
--Ezekiel 22:1-2,6-7 NIV

In chapter 22 of the Book of Jeremiah, the prophet
proclaims judgment on the evil kings of Judah. Verses 13
and 17 are directed at King Jehoiakim, the son of King
Josiah. He acquired his wealth by means of dishonest gain,
extortion, cheating his workers, injustice, oppressing the
poor and weak, and shedding innocent blood. Chapters 6
and 7 of the Book of Micah present a similar charge against
Israel. Chapter 7, verses 2 and 3, portray Israel as a land of
the ungodly, with the rulers, judges, and people with power
taking advantage of the poor and powerless. They too used
violence and bloodshed to gain power and wealth. The
prophet Ezekiel addressed the sins of the city of Jerusalem,
capital of Judah. The people in Jerusalem turned from God
to worship idols, and they committed all kinds of detestable
sins, including the oppression and mistreatment of aliens,
orphans, widows, and other helpless people in their midst.
The princes of Israel (the city leaders) were charged with
shedding blood to gain power and wealth. Note also in
Ezekiel, chapter 22, verse 7, that fathers and mothers were
not honored in Jerusalem; they were treated with contempt.
    The priests in Israel and Judah were responsible for
instructing the people in matters of the Law and rendering
decisions in areas of conflict. Their charge was to interpret
the Mosaic Law and explain it to the people. The priests
were as corrupt, however, as the rulers and other people with
power.

    On the twenty-fourth day of the ninth month, in the
second year of Darius, the word of the LORD came to

the prophet Haggai: "This is what the LORD Almighty says: 'Ask the priests what the law says:'"....
--Haggai 2:10-11 NIV

"And now this admonition is for you, O priests. If you do not listen, and if you do not set your heart to honor my name," says the LORD Almighty, "I will send a curse upon you, and I will curse your blessings. Yes, I have already cursed them, because you have not set your heart to honor me....."For the lips of the priest ought to preserve knowledge, and from his mouth men should seek instruction---because he is the messenger of the LORD Almighty. But you have turned from the way and by your teaching have caused many to stumble; you have violated the covenant with Levi," says the LORD Almighty. "So I have caused you to be despised and humiliated before all the people, because you have not followed my ways but have shown partiality in matters of the law."
--Malachi 2:1-2,7-9 NIV

Hear this, you leaders of the house of Jacob, you rulers of the house of Israel, who despise justice and distort all that is right; who build Zion with bloodshed, and Jerusalem with wickedness. Her leaders judge for a bribe, her priests teach for a price, and her prophets tell fortunes for money. Yet they lean upon the LORD and say, "Is not the LORD among us? No disaster will come upon us."
--Micah 3:9-11 NIV

In the Book of Haggai, the prophet was told by the Lord to ask the priests for the meaning, or interpretation, of the Law. The prophet Malachi charged the priests in Judah with shirking their responsibilities. They were guilty of false teaching, causing others to sin, and they had shown partiality in matters of the Law. Those actions brought God's judgment down on the priests. Chapter 3 of the Book of Micah presents a charge against the rulers, priests, and prophets in Israel and Judah. Included in the despicable practices of the leaders was interpretation of the Law by the priests for a price. If a person suffered a wrong, he or she could go to the priest for a ruling or application of the Law. But, if that person had no money, he or she could not get a hearing before the priest. That was true also for hearings before corrupt judges and prophets.

We have discussed briefly the divine commands and precepts mediated through Moses to govern the overall conduct of God's people, the Israelites. That Mosaic Law is lengthy and very complex, so it is virtually impossible to obey completely. We have also considered the multitude of sins committed by the Israelites over several centuries. But, the question still unanswered is, "What did the Lord expect of His chosen people, Israel?" Let us review four Scripture passages, which I believe shed some light on that key question.

> "I hate, I despise your religious feasts; I cannot stand your assemblies. Even though you bring me burnt offerings and grain offerings, I will not accept them. Though you bring choice fellowship offerings, I will have no regard for them. Away with the noise of your songs! I will not listen to the music of your harps. But let justice roll on like a river, righteousness like a never-failing stream!"
> --Amos 5:21-24 NIV

The prophet Amos called for Israel's repentance for their many sins. Through Amos, the Lord rejected the sacrifices and offerings enumerated in the Mosaic Law, and He despised their feasts and other worship assemblies which were also required by the Law. God refused to listen to their music and songs, which were supposedly offered to Him in praise and thanksgiving. Why did the Lord reject the Israelites' offerings, worship rituals, and praise? I believe it was because He considered them all to be insincere; they were just empty words and actions. The people's sinful conduct indicated their worship of God was superficial and insincere. God did not say the Israelites should refrain from presenting offerings, sacrifices, and praise in worship of Him. He simply said they should change their attitudes and actions before they came before Him in worship.

God does not want halfhearted and insincere worship from His people. Three related Scripture passages tell us what the Lord desires from His people, rather than the legalistic and superficial worship of the Israelites.

> And now, O Israel, what does the LORD your God ask of you but to fear the LORD your God, to walk in his ways, to love him, to serve the LORD your God with all your heart and with all your soul, and to observe the LORD's commands and decrees that I am giving you today for your own good?
> --Deuteronomy 10:12-13 NIV

> And the word of the LORD came again to Zechariah: "This is what the LORD Almighty says: 'Administer true justice; show mercy and compassion to one another. Do not oppress the widow or the fatherless, the alien or the poor. In your hearts do not think evil of each other.'"
> --Zechariah 7:8-10 NIV

> With what shall I come before the LORD and bow down before the exalted God? Shall I come before

him with burnt offerings, with calves a year old? Will
the LORD be pleased with thousands of rams, with ten
thousand rivers of oil? Shall I offer my firstborn for
my transgressions, the fruit of my body for the sin of
my soul? He has showed you, O man, what is good.
And what does the LORD require of you? To act justly
and to love mercy and to walk humbly with your God.
--Micah 6:6-8 NIV

The passage in Deuteronomy tells God's chosen people, and
us as well, to reverence the Lord; that is, to recognize who
He is, to trust in Him, and to commit to Him. God's people
are also told to walk in His ways and love Him. That means
we are to be obedient to Him in all that we do and put Him
first in our lives. We are told further to serve the Lord with
our total being. The Scripture passage in Zechariah
summarizes what the Lord expects from His people with
respect to their relationships with others. We should be fair
and honest, rendering true judgments, always being kind and
compassionate toward others. We are told to watch out for
and help those in our society who are needy and helpless,
and we must not devise evil against one another.

The Scripture passage in the Book of Micah reflects
the real meaning of pure religion, being what God wants us
to be. Acceptance by God cannot be achieved by means of
offerings and sacrifices or any other religious ritual.
Righteous living is the only thing we can do to please the
Lord. Our relationship with God cannot be right if we do
not have right relationships with others. We "act justly" by
being honest and fair with everyone, by protecting the rights
of the weak and helpless people in our midst, and by not
showing favoritism toward the rich and powerful in our
society. We "love mercy" by fulfilling the obligations in
our relationships with others, even when we are not required
to do so, by loving someone simply because of their need to

be loved, and by loving other people sacrificially the way God loved us when He sent His Son to die on a cross for our sins. We can "walk humbly" with God only if we act justly and love mercy in our relationships with one another. Walking humbly with God means we should reverence Him, be obedient to Him, obey His Word, and yield our will to His perfect will.

I believe the Scripture passages in Micah, chapter 6, and Zechariah, chapter 7, express the true meaning of living our lives as God desires. Note that God asks us to change our attitudes and conduct, but He does not demand that we try to change others. That is the Lord's responsibility. We would do well to remember that and apply it in our lives. The passage in Micah reiterates an extremely important Biblical truth. God did not condemn the offerings, sacrifices, and rituals required by the Mosaic Law. Neither did He condemn the Israelites' observance of those external religious activities. What God did condemn was the Israelites' attitudes and actions toward others while they were observing the external religious activities required by the Law. The Lord is more concerned about internal matters, what is in our hearts and how we relate to other people, than He is about legalistic external matters, the observance of religious rituals. We must keep that truth in mind as we establish priorities in our present-day society that will please God.

Chapter 5

What God Desires of His Church

The Old Testament reveals how the Lord dealt with His chosen people, Israel, and what He expected of them. The principles and guidelines for living presented in the Old Testament also applied during New Testament times, and I believe they are relevant to our society today. The universal Church, consisting of believers from all time periods, is now God's people, so I believe the instructions and commands for living included in the New Testament are addressed primarily to the universal Church, local churches, and individual Christians. Join me as we examine pertinent Scripture passages in the New Testament to determine what God desires of His people today, but we must not forget the principles for living presented in the Old Testament.

The religious right and moderate Christians agree that evangelism is the foremost and fundamental calling of all

Christians. We spread the Good News by means of our personal witness, the verbal sharing of our faith and the Gospel with others, and we also spread the Good News by means of our living witness, the way we live our lives. How we conduct ourselves and relate to other people is therefore extremely important, so that is an area we must focus on as we consider the teaching of the New Testament.

We now address the question, "What does God desire of Christians today, what constitutes pure religion?" The people of Israel lived under the Mosaic Law, a legalistic listing of things they could not do and other things they should do. We live under grace in the Christian era, rather than under a legalistic set of commandments and precepts, but we do have the Bible as a guideline for our attitudes and conduct. Our goal is to define pure religion, the way the Lord wants us to live, from the perspective of the New Testament, but to do so in light of Old Testament teaching. Perhaps we can then determine what God desires of His people today and establish priorities for dealing with the many problems and controversial issues in today's society.

Jesus tells us in one of His earliest teachings, the Sermon on the Mount, included in the Book of Matthew, chapters 5-7, that He did not come to abolish the Law and the messages of the prophets, but to fulfill them.

> Now when he saw the crowds, he went up on a mountainside and sat down. His disciples came to him, and he began to teach them, saying:…. "Do not think that I have come to abolish the Law or the Prophets; I have not come to abolish them but to fulfill them."
> --Matthew 5:1-2,17 NIV

This Scripture passage tells us, I believe, that the principles for living presented in the Mosaic Law and the books of the prophets are relevant today. So, that means we must interpret New Testament Scripture in light of Old Testament teaching as we seek to determine how Christians can best please God in today's politicized society.

What was the purpose of God sending His Incarnate Son, Jesus Christ, to dwell with humankind? I am confident we all agree that God's overall purpose was to provide a way to reconcile sinful humankind to Holy God, to offer salvation to all human beings. That was accomplished through Jesus' sacrificial death on the Cross at Calvary and His resurrection from the dead three days later. But, how did Jesus define His own mission?

> He went to Nazareth, where he had been brought up, and on the Sabbath day he went into the synagogue, as was his custom. And he stood up to read. The scroll of the prophet Isaiah was handed to him. Unrolling it, he found the place where it is written: "The Spirit of the Lord is on me, because he has anointed me to preach good news to the poor. He has sent me to proclaim freedom for the prisoners and recovery of sight for the blind, to release the oppressed, to proclaim the year of the Lord's favor." Then he rolled up the scroll, gave it back to the attendant and sat down. The eyes of everyone in the synagogue were fastened on him, and he began by saying to them, "Today this scripture is fulfilled in your hearing."
> --Luke 4:16-21 NIV

> When the men came to Jesus, they said, "John the Baptist sent us to you to ask, 'Are you the one who was to come, or should we expect someone else?'" At that very time Jesus cured many who had diseases, sicknesses and evil spirits, and gave sight to many who were blind. So he replied to the messengers, "Go back

and report to John what you have seen and heard: The blind receive sight, the lame walk, those who have leprosy are cured, the deaf hear, the dead are raised, and the good news is preached to the poor."
--Luke 7:20-22 NIV

Jesus was teaching in a Jewish synagogue soon after His baptism by John the Baptist and His forty-day temptation by Satan in the wilderness. He quoted the prophet Isaiah in that early sermon and stated clearly that His mission included ministry to the physical needs of poor, sick, helpless, and downtrodden people in the society of His day. Messengers from John the Baptist asked Jesus if He was the promised Messiah, and Jesus' response again emphasized that His mission was to help those who could not help themselves.

Jesus taught much more during His three-year earthly ministry, and His disciples, including the Apostle Paul, clarified and expanded His teaching. In addition, Jesus' life and ministry sets forth a perfect example for Christians to emulate. That means Christians today must minister to the physical needs of the helpless, sick, oppressed, and downtrodden in our society. We must carry on the Jesus agenda. Today's society is much more complex than that of Jesus' day, but our mission remains the same as His. We must not forget that important Biblical truth as we endeavor to establish priorities for Christians in America today.

Jesus' Sermon on the Mount informs us that He is more concerned about our attitudes and what is in our hearts than He is about our conduct. Our actions are the result of our internal attitudes, thoughts, biases, priorities, emotions, and motivations. If our heart is truly right, our conduct will be right as well.

"You have heard that it was said to the people long ago, 'Do not murder, and anyone who murders will be

subject to judgment.' But I tell you that anyone who is angry with his brother will be subject to judgment....."You have heard that it was said, 'Do not commit adultery.' But I tell you that anyone who looks at a woman lustfully has already committed adultery with her in his heart."
--Matthew 5:21-22a,27-28 NIV

"But the things that come out of the mouth come from the heart, and these make a man 'unclean.' For out of the heart come evil thoughts, murder, adultery, sexual immorality, theft, false testimony, slander. These are what make a man 'unclean;'...."
--Matthew 15:18-20a NIV

Jesus is not saying He is unconcerned about the things we say and do. He is simply telling us our external conduct depends on the condition of our heart, and that if our heart is right, our speech and actions will be right.

The Ten Commandments in the Old Testament are the foundation upon which all the provisions of the Mosaic Law are structured. The first four commandments govern our relationship with God, and the last six speak to our relationships with others. Jesus condensed those Ten Commandments even more in the New Testament.

One of them, an expert in the law, tested him with this question: "Teacher, which is the greatest commandment in the law?" Jesus replied: "' Love the Lord your God with all your heart and with all your soul and with all your mind.' This is the first and greatest commandment. And the second is like it: 'Love your neighbor as yourself.' All the Law and the Prophets hang on these two commandments."
--Matthew 22:35-40 NIV

First and foremost, God demands that we love, reverence, and obey Him with our entire being. If our relationship with God is not right, we cannot relate to others in the right way. The second commandment is that we love our neighbor, and in the context of this Scripture passage, "neighbor" is anyone we come in contact with, both people we like and those we dislike. The "love" we must have for our neighbor is a love that seeks what is best for him or her, regardless of the cost to self, a sacrificial love exemplified by Jesus Christ when He gave His life on a cross to atone for our sins. All the detailed instructions and precepts included in the Old Testament hang on those two commandments.

The two commandments given by Jesus raise an interesting question. "Which is more important, worshiping God or having right relationships with one another?" Jesus answered that question in His Sermon on the Mount.

> "Therefore, if you are offering your gift at the altar and there remember that your brother has something against you, leave your gift there in front of the altar. First go and be reconciled to your brother; then come and offer your gift."
> --Matthew 5:23-24 NIV

When we come to worship God ("offering your gift at the altar") and remember we have offended another Christian in some way ("your brother has something against you"), we must first go and be reconciled to that person we have offended. Then, we can worship God. I believe this Scripture passage teaches us that it is impossible to truly worship God if we do not have right relationships with one another. Or, stated another way, having right relationships with others demonstrates a right relationship with the Lord.

The Apostle Paul admonishes us to live by the indwelling Holy Spirit who is present with all Christians. He speaks of an ongoing internal warfare between our inherently sinful human nature and the indwelling Spirit of God. Paul's teaching about a Spirit-led life is summarized in a Scripture passage from the Book of Galatians.

> So I say, live by the Spirit, and you will not gratify the desires of the sinful nature. For the sinful nature desires what is contrary to the Spirit, and the Spirit what is contrary to the sinful nature. They are in conflict with each other, so that you do not do what you want. But if you are led by the Spirit, you are not under law. The acts of the sinful nature are obvious: sexual immorality, impurity and debauchery; idolatry and witchcraft; hatred, discord, jealousy, fits of rage, selfish ambition, dissensions, factions and envy; drunkenness, orgies, and the like. I warn you, as I did before, that those who live like this will not inherit the kingdom of God. But the fruit of the Spirit is love, joy, peace, patience, kindness, goodness, faithfulness, gentleness and self-control. Against such things there is no law. Those who belong to Christ Jesus have crucified the sinful nature with its passions and desires. Since we live by the Spirit, let us keep in step with the Spirit. Let us not become conceited, provoking and envying each other.
> --Galations 5:16-26 NIV

In this passage, Paul presents a contrast between a life controlled by our sinful human nature and a life controlled by the indwelling Holy Spirit. These are referred to as the works of the flesh and the works of the Spirit, and they involve our physical deeds, our inner attitudes, and our social relationships. Included in works of the flesh are sexual misconduct (sexual immorality, impurity, and debauchery) and sinful religious practices (idolatry and witchcraft). The works of the flesh also involve sinful conflicts and wrong attitudes in our social relationships (hatred, discord, jealousy, fits of rage, selfish ambitions, dissensions, factions, and envy). Disagreements in our social relationships are not necessarily bad, provided they do not lead to dislike and ill feelings toward one another; we should agree to disagree. Paul's works of the flesh include out-of-control and unrestrained pleasure seeking (drunkenness and orgies). He ended his list of the works of the flesh with "and the like" to indicate the list is not exhaustive. A life controlled by our evil human nature leads to all kinds of sinful behavior and wrong attitudes.

In contrast to the works of the flesh, the works of the Spirit (or fruit of the Spirit) lead to a life that is pleasing to God. The fruit of the Spirit are nine inner qualities produced by the Holy Spirit working in a Christian's life. In essence, it is the character of the Spirit of God showing forth in the life of a believer. The observing world sees the Holy Spirit in the life of an obedient Christian. The nine virtues of the Spirit, namely love, joy, peace, patience, kindness, goodness, faithfulness, gentleness, and self-control, are internalized in a believer. But, those internal attributes do affect the external behavior of a Christian, and they affect his or her relationship with others as well. The challenge for us, therefore, is to live by the Spirit, rather than under the control of our sinful human nature. All of us have that ongoing spiritual warfare within us between the Holy Spirit and our evil human nature, so we must yield to the Spirit's control of our lives. The more we do that, the more pleasing our lives are to the Lord.

A number of other Scripture passages in the New Testament warn us about sinful activities and attitudes. Some of those sins may seem more grievous to us than others, but we must remember that God hates all sin; sin is sin in God's eyes, and any sin we commit displeases Him. We have a tendency to magnify the sins of others and consider our transgressions to be just "little sins."

> Do you not know that the wicked will not inherit the kingdom of God? Do not be deceived: Neither the sexually immoral nor idolaters nor adulterers nor male prostitutes nor homosexual offenders nor thieves nor the greedy nor drunkards nor slanderers nor swindlers will inherit the kingdom of God.
> --1 Corinthians 6:9-10 NIV

> Do not let any unwholesome talk come out of your mouths, but only what is helpful for building others up according to their needs, that it may benefit those who listen. And do not grieve the Holy Spirit of God, with whom you were sealed for the day of redemption. Get rid of all bitterness, rage and anger, brawling and slander, along with every form of malice. Be kind and compassionate to one another, forgiving each other, just as in Christ God forgave you.
> --Ephesians 4:29-32 NIV

> Finally, all of you, live in harmony with one another; be sympathetic, love as brothers, be compassionate and humble. Do not repay evil with evil or insult with insult, but with blessing, because to this you were called so that you may inherit a blessing.
> --1 Peter 3:8-9 NIV

Adulterers, prostitutes, and homosexuals are listed as sinners in the passage from 1 Corinthians. But, are they any more evil than thieves, greedy people, slanderers, and swindlers? What about the wealthy individual who cheats on his or her income taxes and thus steals from our government, and from us? Or the chief executive of a large corporation who reduces or eliminates employee retirement benefits and therefore swindles the corporation's employees out of promised retirement income? And, what about the individuals, political campaigns, political action committees, and other special-interest groups that spread misrepresentations, innuendos, and untruths about other people or opposition political candidates? Is that not slander? The greedy includes a wide range of sinners; those who covet money and power, those who take advantage of the poor and helpless for personal gain, those who engage in price gouging, those who covet material possessions, and so forth. We must be careful about trying to rank-order sinful activities and behavior.

The passage in the Book of Ephesians, chapter 4, focuses on our relationships with other people. The emphasis is on unwholesome speech, that which hurts others, and the internal attitudes expressed in that hurtful speech. Believers are commanded to get rid of such sinful attitudes and replace them with attitudes of kindness, compassion, and forgiveness. We are told in 1 Peter, chapter 3, verses 8-9, to live in harmony with others, and to relate to one another with love, compassion, sympathy, and humility. This passage instructs us not to retaliate when we believe we have been wronged in some way; we are told to forgive those who wronged us instead. We are admonished throughout the New Testament to "put off" all sinful attitudes and behavior and to "put on" virtuous attitudes and conduct, those attributes derived from the fruit of the Spirit.

Let us consider briefly a number of other sinful and hurtful attitudes which adversely affect our relationships with one another. Favoritism, or partiality, involves preferential treatment of someone because of who they are. Such partiality toward an individual or a people group can be because of race, nationality, economic class, social status, or similar factors.

> Then Peter began to speak: "I now realize how true it is that God does not show favoritism but accepts men from every nation who fear him and do what is right."
> --Acts 10:34-35 NIV

> "Do not pervert justice; do not show partiality to the poor or favoritism to the great, but judge your neighbor fairly."
> --Leviticus 19:15 NIV

> My brothers, as believers in our glorious Lord Jesus Christ, don't show favoritism.....If you really keep the royal law found in Scripture, "Love your neighbor as yourself," you are doing right. But if you show favoritism, you sin and are convicted by the law as lawbreakers. For whoever keeps the whole law and yet stumbles at just one point is guilty of breaking all of it.....Speak and act as those who are going to be judged by the law that gives freedom, because judgment without mercy will be shown to anyone who has not been merciful. Mercy triumphs over judgment!
> --James 2:1,8-10,12-13 NIV

The passage in Acts, chapter 10, informs us that God is no respecter of persons, that He does not show favoritism toward anyone, and that He accepts any person who reveres Him, regardless of where that person is from or his or her station in life. Leviticus, chapter 19, verse 15, commanded the people of Israel, and us as well, to be fair and just to everyone, not showing partiality. That particular passage is included in the Mosaic Law given by the Lord through

Moses. James, the half-brother of Jesus, tells us not to show favoritism, and he warns us that if we do show partiality we are sinning by disobeying the Law. He goes on to inform us that disobeying only one point of the Law makes us guilty of breaking the whole Law. The "royal law" referred to by James is the basic law, the source of all other laws pertaining to human relationships. The bottom line is, "Showing favoritism is a sin, and it displeases God."

Self-righteousness is an attitude whereby we consider ourselves to be better than others; we place ourselves on spiritual pedestals. The Pharisees in the New Testament were guilty of being self-righteous, and Jesus came down hard on them because of that attitude of superiority. In essence, we are judging others when we consider them to be spiritually inferior to us.

> "Two men went up to the temple to pray, one a Pharisee and the other a tax collector. The Pharisee stood up and prayed about himself: 'God, I thank you that I am not like other men---robbers, evildoers, adulterers---or even like this tax collector. I fast twice a week and give a tenth of all I get.' "But the tax collector stood at a distance. He would not even look up to heaven, but beat his breast and said, 'God, have mercy on me, a sinner.' "I tell you that this man, rather than the other, went home justified before God. For everyone who exalts himself will be humbled, and he who humbles himself will be exalted."
> --Luke 18:10-14 NIV

> "Woe to you Pharisees, because you give God a tenth of your mint, rue and all other kinds of garden herbs, but you neglect justice and the love of God. You should have practiced the latter without leaving the former undone. Woe to you Pharisees, because you

love the most important seats in the synagogues and greetings in the marketplaces.
--Luke 11:42-43 NIV

"Woe to you, teachers of the law and Pharisees, you hypocrites! You clean the outside of the cup and dish, but inside they are full of greed and self-indulgence. Blind Pharisees! First clean the inside of the cup and dish, and then the outside also will be clean."
--Matthew 23:25-26 NIV

The pious Pharisee in Luke, chapter 18, considered himself to be spiritually superior to those he classified as sinners, namely the robbers, evildoers, adulterers, and tax collectors. He even boasted about fasting and tithing. On the other hand, the humble tax collector recognized himself as a sinner and asked God for mercy. Jesus' response tells us clearly He is displeased by self-righteousness; He wants us to come before Him humbly and with reverence. Note in Luke, chapter 11, that Jesus charged the Pharisees with neglecting justice, not being fair and honest with others. Not only does an attitude of self-righteousness affect our relationship with the Lord, it is also damaging in our relationships with other people. The Scripture passage in Matthew, chapter 23, reiterates the teaching in Luke about self-righteousness. The morality and righteousness of the Pharisees were superficial, depending on external rituals and actions demanded by the Law. What God really wants from His people are those internal virtues derived from His indwelling Spirit, attributes that are manifested in our sincere love and reverence of Him, together with right relationships with others.

Self-righteousness leads to another sinful attitude, that of judging others. The Bible teaches clearly that God alone can judge people, that we must refrain from judging one another. We are not talking about judgments rendered through our judicial system and supported by the laws of our land. We are referring to our judgments of others because they have different value systems, approve of behavior we consider to be sinful, have different religious or political views, or just may be different from us. Numerous Scripture passages deal with judging others, but let us consider just two of them.

"Do not judge, or you too will be judged. For in the same way you judge others, you will be judged, and with the measure you use, it will be measured to you. "Why do you look at the speck of sawdust in your brother's eye and pay no attention to the plank in your own eye? How can you say to your brother, 'Let me take the speck out of your eye,' when all the time there is a plank in your own eye? You hypocrite, first take the plank out of your own eye, and then you will see clearly to remove the speck from your brother's eye." --Matthew 7:1-5 NIV

You, therefore, have no excuse, you who pass judgment on someone else, for at whatever point you judge the other, you are condemning yourself, because you who pass judgment do the same things. Now we know that God's judgment against those who do such things is based on truth. So when you, a mere man, pass judgment on them and yet do the same things, do you think you will escape God's judgment? Or do you show contempt for the riches of his kindness, tolerance and patience, not realizing that God's kindness leads you toward repentance? But because of your stubbornness and your unrepentant heart, you are storing up wrath against yourself for the day of God's wrath, when his righteous judgment will be revealed.

> God will "give to each person according to what he has
> done."
> --Romans 2:1-6 NIV

When we judge others, we are in essence attempting to impose our moral beliefs and value systems on them. The passage in Matthew, chapter 7, is from Jesus' Sermon on the Mount. He is not referring to a gentle and loving confrontation of someone who is perhaps caught in an obvious sin or wrongdoing. Jesus is talking about self-righteous criticism or condemnation of another person for their actions or conduct. That passage warns us we must not criticize another person for a small failing while we harbor a much larger fault in our own lives. We are too often guilty of ignoring or minimizing our own transgressions as we amplify the faults of others. Jesus assures us that when we judge others harshly and without love, God will judge us with the same severity.

The passage in Romans, chapter 2, has a similar message. In chapter 1 of his letter to the Roman church, the Apostle Paul characterized the sinful and immoral lifestyle of the pagans, or Gentiles, those who had a limited revelation of God. He described the Lord's judgment on the pagan society because of their immorality, their rejection of God, and their arrogance. Then, in chapter 2, Paul confronted the Jews, those who had a deeper knowledge of God, a greater awareness of sin, and an understanding of God's judgment on sin. The Jews applauded God's judgment of the Gentiles, but they were just as guilty of disobeying the Lord and were practicing the same kinds of sins. Paul told the Jews, and he tells us, not to judge others for what we deem to be their faults, because we have the same degree of sin in our lives. Paul has strong words for those who do pass judgment on others. They show contempt for God's kindness, tolerance, and patience, and because of their stubbornness and unrepentant hearts, they are storing up wrath against themselves for the day of God's judgment at the end of time. All these and other similar warnings in Scripture make it crystal clear. We must not judge one another; if we do, it is a sin.

We are all guilty of another sin, the sin of omission. We tend to interpret sin as doing something we are forbidden to do, and we relate righteousness to not doing those forbidden things. However, the Bible tells us that not doing what we know we should do is equally as wrong.

> Anyone, then, who knows the good he ought to do and doesn't do it, sins.
> --James 4:17 NIV

Not forgiving someone who has wronged us is a sin. Not showing kindness, compassion, and mercy toward others, even those who are different from us, is a sin. Not helping someone in need is a sin. Not standing up for the weak and helpless in our society is a sin. Not providing equal education and employment opportunities for all our citizens is a sin. In essence, not allowing the fruit of the Spirit to be manifested in and through our lives is sinning against God.

People in our culture, including Christians, strive for wealth and power. One's success in our society is often measured by the amount of material possessions he or she accumulates. Possessing significant wealth and a lot of "things" may boost an individual's pride and self-esteem, resulting in a feeling of self-sufficiency, but does that attitude please God? A passage in the Book of Deuteronomy answers clearly that question.

> "For the LORD your God is bringing you into a good land, a land of brooks of water, of fountains and springs, flowing forth in valleys and hills; a land of

wheat and barley, of vines and fig trees and pomegranates, a land of olive oil and honey; a land where you shall eat food without scarcity, in which you shall not lack anything; a land whose stones are iron, and out of whose hills you can dig copper. "When you have eaten and are satisfied, you shall bless the LORD your God for the good land which He has given you. "Beware lest you forget the LORD your God by not keeping His commandments and His ordinances and His statutes which I am commanding you today; lest, when you have eaten and are satisfied, and have built good houses and lived in them, and when your herds and your flocks multiply, and your silver and gold multiply, and all that you have multiplies, then your heart becomes proud, and you forget the LORD your God who brought you out from the land of Egypt, out of the house of slavery….."Otherwise, you may say in your heart, 'My power and the strength of my hand made me this wealth.' "But you shall remember the LORD your God, for it is He who is giving you power to make wealth, that He may confirm His covenant which He swore to your fathers, as it is this day.
--Deuteronomy 8:7-14,17-18 NAS

The Israelites were preparing to enter the Promised Land of Canaan after forty years of wandering in the wilderness between Egypt and Canaan. This passage in Deuteronomy is included in Moses' farewell address to his people, wherein he reiterated the goodness of the land the Lord was giving them and warned them about wrong attitudes and conduct once they were settled in Canaan.

The Israelites in Moses' day, just like many Christians today, were quick to claim credit for their prosperity. Our human tendency is to attribute success to either hard work on our part or greater wisdom we claim to possess. Such an egotistical attitude displeases God. He wants us to depend on Him and to acknowledge Him as the source of all our material blessings. The Lord tested the Israelites during their forty years of wandering in the wilderness to teach them humility and to teach them to depend on Him for all their needs. Christians today also need to recognize that the Lord is the source of their good fortune. Our power and ability to gain wealth comes from God, and we must never look down on or criticize those who are less fortunate. Humility is a virtue God desires for all His people.

President Abraham Lincoln believed the Civil War was the result of God's judgment on America. He issued a proclamation on April 30, 1863, in which he wrote: "We have forgotten the gracious hand which preserved us in peace, and multiplied and enriched and strengthened us. And have vainly imagined in the deceitfulness of our hearts that all these blessings were produced by some superior wisdom and virtue of our own. Intoxicated with unbroken success, we have become too self-sufficient to feel the necessity of redeeming and preserving grace, too proud to pray to the God that made us." The Israelites of Moses' time had an attitude of pride and self-exaltation. Americans in the era of President Lincoln shared that same attitude, and Christians today are no different. We have not learned true humility.

Perhaps we are now equipped to define pure religion, a lifestyle that God desires of His people, in light of the teaching of both the Old Testament and the New Testament. We determined what God expected of His chosen people, Israel, in a previous chapter of this book, and we concluded that Old Testament principles of living apply to us today. We considered Jesus' definition of His own mission to help the poor and afflicted in His day, and we concluded that Jesus is more concerned about the condition of our hearts and our attitudes than He is about our actions. If our hearts are right, our conduct will be right.

The Apostle Paul and other writers of the New Testament stress the importance of those internal attributes resulting from the work of the Holy Spirit in our lives. That fruit of the Spirit manifests itself in right relationships with others. We also identified a number of undesirable attitudes and actions that can be harmful in our relationships with one another. Allowing the Holy Spirit to guide and control our lives is the key to a fruitful life for God and right relationships with others. But, allowing one's sinful human nature to be in control leads to a life that displeases God.

Passages from Old Testament Books of Zechariah and Micah summarize what the Lord expects of His people with regard to both their relationship with Him and their relationships with others.

And the word of the LORD came again to Zechariah: "This is what the LORD Almighty says: 'Administer true justice; show mercy and compassion to one another. Do not oppress the widow or the fatherless, the alien or the poor. In your hearts do not think evil of each other.'"
--Zechariah 7:8-10 NIV

With what shall I come before the LORD and bow down before the exalted God? Shall I come before him with burnt offerings, with calves a year old? Will the LORD be pleased with thousands of rams, with ten thousand rivers of oil? Shall I offer my firstborn for my transgressions, the fruit of my body for the sin of my soul? He has showed you, O man, what is good. And what does the LORD require of you? To act justly and to love mercy and to walk humbly with your God.
--Micah 6:6-8 NIV

God wants us to walk in humble fellowship with Him, reverencing and worshiping Him, being obedient to His Word, and yielding our imperfect will to His perfect will. The Lord desires that His people be fair, honest, and just with everyone. That includes both our personal relationships with others and our standing up for the rights of the poor, weak, and helpless in our society. The Lord also wants us to relate to one another with love, kindness, compassion, and mercy, especially in our treatment of those who cannot help themselves.

One key verse of Scripture in the New Testament sheds additional light on the meaning of pure religion. That verse of Scripture from the Book of James is significant in that it tells us explicitly what is required in pure religion, and it tells us implicitly what is not included.

> Religion that God our Father accepts as pure and faultless is this: to look after orphans and widows in their distress and to keep oneself from being polluted by the world.
> --James 1:27 NIV

The pure religion defined by James is a practical religion, a religion carried out through our day-to-day relationships with other people. He admonishes us to touch people's lives and to minister to them in the world in which they live. It involves our willing treatment and care for the poor, needy, and helpless in our society, thus reflecting our concern and compassion for others. Pure religion also involves our lifestyle, what we say and do. We are to have moral and upright lifestyles, not contaminated by the immorality, corruption, and wickedness in the world around us. Implicit in James' definition of pure religion, I believe, is what it does not include. It does not include our trying to change others. We must not try to judge other people, confronting them with a self-righteous attitude, and trying to impose our moral beliefs and value systems on them. That means we must be tolerant of other people's religious and moral beliefs and respect their right to be "different" from us.

Old Testament Scripture tells us God is more concerned about our compassionate and just treatment of the downtrodden members of our society than He is about external religious rituals and expressions. In the New Testament, Jesus defined His mission, the Jesus agenda, as a ministry to the poor, sick, helpless, and oppressed in our midst. The Apostle Paul, Jesus' half-brother, James, and other writers of the New Testament confirmed the importance of good and helpful relationships with other people. The teaching of the entire Word of God thus confirms and supports the Jesus agenda, so I believe it behooves all Christians to place the highest priority on ministry to the poor, sick, weak, and oppressed in our society. Such a ministry enhances our primary mission, that of evangelism, and I believe that is the ministry priority most pleasing to God.

Chapter 6

Jesus Christ and Hypocrites

The basic definition of a hypocrite is a person who professes to be something he or she is not, one who claims to possess attributes or beliefs he or she does not have. A hypocrite is quite often convinced he or she does indeed possess those claimed virtues and attributes. For purposes of this study, however, let us define a hypocrite as a Christian who professes faithful obedience to the teaching of the entire Bible, yet in reality is one who ignores a number of important Biblical mandates. Such a believer clings to strong beliefs about particular issues in our society and turns to selected Scripture passages to support those preconceived views. At the same time, that person ignores Biblical teaching pertaining to issues for which he or she has little concern. We refer to that form of Scripture application as picking and choosing which parts of the Bible to obey. We must recognize, however, that all of us are guilty of hypocrisy to some extent. Each of us tends to emphasize those Scripture passages which seem to justify our views on key social issues, but we oftentimes give only lip service to passages which support beliefs different from ours on other issues.

Jesus had to deal with hypocrites during His three-year earthly ministry. The most obvious hypocrites in Jesus' day were the Pharisees, a Jewish religious sect who believed in strict adherence to the Mosaic Law. They were considered to be the most learned and religious laymen in the first century A.D. Not only were the Pharisees guardian of the written Law in the Old Testament, they also adhered to numerous oral traditions accumulated and passed down from generation to generation. Those traditions were oral interpretations of the first five books of the Old Testament, and they had been developed and redefined over many generations. The purpose of those oral traditions was to apply the Mosaic Law to all aspects of Jewish life, but they had become extremely complex and burdensome to the Jewish people. Actually, the Pharisees were guilty of using the oral traditions as a means of circumventing the basic requirements of the Law, justifying in their minds disobedience of the Law. The Pharisees possessed spiritual authority in Jewish culture with regard to public worship practices, spiritual cleansing, sacrificial offerings, public prayers, and various other ritualistic practices. By placing so much emphasis on oral traditions, the Pharisees were essentially teaching human traditions as God's Law.

The Pharisees practiced their own brand of religious fundamentalism, that of trying to impose their interpretations of the Law, in combination with oral traditions, on the Jewish people, quite often for personal gain. Needless to say, Jesus came down hard on the

Pharisees, with "hypocrites" being His most common characterization of them.

> The Pharisees and some teachers of the law who had come from Jerusalem gathered around Jesus and saw some of his disciples eating food with hands that were "unclean," that is, unwashed. (The Pharisees and all the Jews do not eat unless they give their hands a ceremonial washing, holding to the tradition of the elders. When they come from the marketplace they do not eat unless they wash. And they observe many other traditions, such as the washing of cups, pitchers and kettles.) So the Pharisees and teachers of the law asked Jesus, "Why don't your disciples live according to the tradition of the elders instead of eating their food with 'unclean' hands?" He replied, "Isaiah was right when he prophesied about you hypocrites; as it is written: 'These people honor me with their lips, but their hearts are far from me. They worship me in vain; their teachings are but rules taught by men.' You have let go of the commands of God and are holding on to the traditions of men." And he said to them: "You have a fine way of setting aside the commands of God in order to observe your own traditions! For Moses said, 'Honor your father and your mother,' and, 'Anyone who curses his father or mother must be put to death.' But you say that if a man says to his father or mother: 'Whatever help you might otherwise have received from me is Corban' (that is, a gift devoted to God), then you no longer let him do anything for his father or mother. Thus you nullify the word of God by your tradition that you have handed down. And you do many things like that."
> --Mark 7:1-13 NIV

> Meanwhile, when a crowd of many thousands had gathered, so that they were trampling on one another, Jesus began to speak first to his disciples, saying: "Be on your guard against the yeast of the Pharisees, which is hypocrisy."
> --Luke 12:1 NIV

The word "Pharisees" means separated ones, with the implication being separation from anything unholy or spiritually unclean so they would be fit to serve the Lord. But, the Pharisees had developed an extensive set of instructions pertaining to external cleanliness, or holiness, and they had ignored the need for internal cleansing. They set forth meticulous rituals and ceremonial laws regarding hand washing before a meal, cleansing cooking utensils, and cleansing their bodies after touching someone or something "unclean." The traditions of the Pharisees were man-made laws that were in contradiction to the intent of the Mosaic Law.

In the passage from Mark, chapter 7, the Pharisees confronted Jesus about the way His disciples ate with unclean hands. They had not given their hands a ceremonial washing according to the traditions of the Pharisees. The Pharisees were concerned about ritualistic external cleansing rather than the internal condition of the heart; their priority was wrong. Jesus referred to the Pharisees as hypocrites and gave an example of their hypocrisy. The Law demanded that the Israelites honor their fathers and mothers, meaning they must provide them with financial support when needed. But, the Pharisees developed traditions enabling them to circumvent that requirement of the Law. They could declare their financial resources as "Corban," a gift devoted to God, and then they would not be required to use those resources to support their parents. Jesus accused the Pharisees of nullifying God's commands by their many traditions. We see in Luke, chapter 12, verse 1, Jesus warning His disciples about the hypocrisy of the Pharisees.

Another point of contention between the Pharisees and Jesus was how the Sabbath should be observed, an important concern for the Jews. The Pharisees had formulated their own strict requirements for observing the Sabbath. One of their requirements was that work could not be performed on the Sabbath, and they had made a long and detailed list of what constituted work.

One Sabbath Jesus was going through the grainfields, and his disciples began to pick some heads of grain, rub them in their hands and eat the kernels. Some of the Pharisees asked, "Why are you doing what is unlawful on the Sabbath?" Jesus answered them, "Have you never read what David did when he and his companions were hungry? He entered the house of God, and taking the consecrated bread, he ate what is lawful only for the priests to eat. And he also gave some to his companions." Then Jesus said to them, "The Son of Man is Lord of the Sabbath." On another Sabbath he went into the synagogue and was teaching, and a man was there whose right hand was shriveled. The Pharisees and the teachers of the Law were looking for a reason to accuse Jesus, so they watched him closely to see if he would heal on the Sabbath. But Jesus knew what they were thinking and said to the man with the shriveled hand, "Get up and stand in front of everyone." So he got up and stood there. Then Jesus said to them, "I ask you, which is lawful on the Sabbath: to do good or to do evil, to save life or to destroy it?" He looked around at them all, and then said to the man, "Stretch out your hand." He did so, and his hand was completely restored. But they were

furious and began to discuss with one another what
they might do to Jesus.
--Luke 6:1-11 NIV

Then he said to them, "The Sabbath was made for
man, not man for the Sabbath. So the Son of Man is
Lord even of the Sabbath."
--Mark 2:27 NIV

Picking grain was not one of the tasks allowed by the
Pharisees on the Sabbath, therefore they confronted Jesus
when His disciples began doing so. Jesus reminded the
Pharisees of the time in the Old Testament when David and
his companions took consecrated bread from the house of
God to satisfy their desperate hunger. Eating consecrated
bread was normally considered unlawful, but doing so
would be lawful if it was done for good. God established
the Sabbath for the good of humankind, to allow people to
rest on the seventh day; they would not be required to work
on the Sabbath. Jesus' point was that doing good works is
always in season. The Pharisees even believed it was
unlawful to heal someone on the Sabbath if their life was not
at risk. Jesus healed the man with the crippled hand to again
demonstrate that doing good deeds on the Sabbath was
permissible, but the Pharisees were furious because they
considered such healing on the Sabbath to be unlawful.
Jesus told the Pharisees in the passage from Mark, chapter 2,
that the Sabbath was established for the good of man, not
man for the Sabbath. That is a truth the Pharisees did not
comprehend.

Spiritual cleansing and observance of the Sabbath were
just two of the numerous points of contention between Jesus
and the Pharisees. We find the Pharisees clashing with
Jesus throughout the first four books of the New Testament,
the four Gospels. Three passages of Scripture indicate the

extent of the Pharisees' self-righteousness, arrogance, hypocrisy, selfishness, and animosity toward Jesus.

> "Woe to you, teachers of the law and Pharisees, you hypocrites! You give a tenth of your spices---mint, dill and cummin. But you have neglected the more important matters of the law---justice, mercy and faithfulness. You should have practiced the latter, without neglecting the former. You blind guides! You strain out a gnat but swallow a camel. "Woe to you, teachers of the law and Pharisees, you hypocrites! You clean the outside of the cup and dish, but inside they are full of greed and self-indulgence. Blind Pharisees! First clean the inside of the cup and dish, and then the outside also will be clean."
> --Matthew 23:23-26 NIV

> The Pharisees, who loved money, heard all this and were sneering at Jesus. He said to them, "You are the ones who justify yourselves in the eyes of men, but God knows your hearts. What is highly valued among men is detestable in God's sight."
> --Luke 16:14-15 NIV

> When Jesus left there, the Pharisees and the teachers of the law began to oppose him fiercely and to besiege him with questions, waiting to catch him in something he might say.
> --Luke 11:53-54 NIV

Jesus criticized the Pharisees for emphasizing the external legalistic provisions of the Law, while neglecting the more important internal matters. The Pharisees had carefully obeyed the Law's requirements for tithing, ritualistic cleansing, public worship practices, observance of the

Sabbath, and other such external matters. But, they had ignored the inner qualities demanded by the Law, namely justice, mercy, and faithfulness, among others. Note that Jesus did not rebuke or condemn the Pharisees for following the Law regarding external matters; He simply admonished them for placing a higher priority in those areas. Jesus wanted the Pharisees, and us, to demonstrate the very important internal virtues and attributes in our relationships with God and in our relationships with others. Jesus told the Pharisees in Luke, chapter 16, that they were more concerned about being deemed righteous by people than they were about being acceptable in God's eyes. The Pharisees tried continually to find ways to discredit Jesus, even to the point of finding justification for putting Him to death. They followed Jesus around waiting to catch Him in something He might say or do.

The Pharisees, the most religious sect of the Jews, were the ones Jesus came down the hardest on in the New Testament. That tells us religious and righteous are not necessarily the same in God's eyes. We must be extremely careful how we view others, not allowing hypocrisy, self-righteousness, arrogance, pride, and selfishness to creep into our attitude toward other people. Instead, we must manifest the fruit of the Spirit, those nine internal virtues, in our relationships with one another. That is the best way we can please God.

One vital Biblical truth emerges from the record of Jesus' dealings with the Pharisees. The Bible may prohibit a particular activity by us or call us to perform some other activity, but that does not necessarily mean those commands are the prevailing instructions in God's Word. We must consider the total teaching of Scripture, putting everything in the proper context, if we truly want to live our lives in a manner that is pleasing to God. Both the Old Testament and the New Testament teach us clearly that our attitudes and actions toward others, especially the weak and helpless in our society, are of utmost importance to God, much more so than following legalistic and ritualistic practices delineated in Scripture. It behooves us to keep that very important truth in mind as we attempt to establish priorities for Christians in our society today.

Chapter 7

Setting Christian Priorities

We have defined the mainstream agenda of the religious right and summarized the overall priorities of moderate Christians. The Old Testament tells us God wanted His chosen people, Israel, to help and stand up for the weak and helpless in their society. Helping people who could not help themselves was to have a higher priority for the Israelites than meeting the ritualistic and legalistic demands of the Mosaic Law. Through Moses and the prophets, God told the Israelites that external matters such as sacrifices, religious feasts, observance of the Sabbath, spiritual cleansing, dietary restrictions, tithing, and other religious rituals were less important than internal matters, their attitude toward, and treatment of, other people. God wanted the Israelites to show mercy and compassion toward the downtrodden and oppressed people in their midst.

The New Testament has a similar message for God's people today, the Church. Jesus Christ defined His own mission, the Jesus agenda, as a ministry to the poor, weak, helpless, and oppressed in the society of His day. We concluded that Jesus expects His universal Church, comprised of all individual Christians, to carry on His mission. We do that with a ministry of compassion toward the afflicted in our society. We too must place a higher priority on internal matters, our attitude toward, and resulting actions to help, the poor, weak, oppressed, and helpless segments of our society. The Bible tells us that if our hearts are truly right our actions will be right as well.

Let us now apply Biblical teaching to the moral and social agenda of social conservatives and to the social ministry priorities of moderate Christians. To do so, I believe we must examine some of the individual issues which are most controversial. Remember, though, that the purpose of our study is not to determine who is right and who is wrong on each of the issues. Our goal is to define overall Christian priorities consistent with Scripture, and thus most pleasing to God. We must consider the individual issues in light of the overall teaching of Scripture. Just because one's position on a particular matter is supported by the Bible does not necessarily mean that issue should have the highest priority in the grand scheme of Christian work and ministry. Our intent is to follow Biblical guidelines as we determine Christian priorities for today's politicized society.

Abortion is the most controversial and the most divisive religious and moral issue facing Christians today. It is both a religious matter and a constitutional concern. One significant area of contention is the point in time when an embryo becomes a person. The question is, "From the time of conception to the time of birth, when does an embryo become a person subject to our nation's laws regarding murder?" The Bible does not mention abortion, but the religious right interprets a Scripture passage in the Book of Psalms so as to define a fetus in the mother's womb as a person. And in their view, taking that fetus' life, an abortion, constitutes murder.

> For thou didst form my inward parts; Thou didst weave me in my mother's womb. I will give thanks to Thee, for I am fearfully and wonderfully made; Wonderful are Thy works, And my soul knows it very well. My frame was not hidden from Thee, When I was made in secret, And skillfully wrought in the depths of the earth. Thine eyes have seen my unformed substance; And in Thy book they were all written, The days that were ordained for me, When as yet there was not one of them.
> --Psalm 139:13-16 NAS

This Scripture passage and one of the Ten Commandments, "You shall not murder." (NAS) form the Biblical basis on which Pro-Lifers derive their belief about abortion. They maintain abortion is murder and thus should be illegal. A significant number of moderate Christians and non-Christians share that view as well, although many of them make exceptions for certain circumstances surrounding a pregnancy.

A majority of moderate Christians and many unbelievers maintain that abortions should be allowed, although most of them believe some restrictions should apply. A number of those Pro-Choice adherents cite a passage in the Book of Exodus to support their view that an abortion does not constitute murder, that a fetus is not a person until after birth.

"And if men struggle with each other and strike a woman with child so that she has a miscarriage, yet there is no further injury, he shall surely be fined as the woman's husband may demand of him; and he shall pay as the judges decide. But if there is any further injury, then you shall appoint as a penalty life for life, eye for eye, tooth for tooth, hand for hand, foot for foot, burn for burn, wound for wound, bruise for bruise."
--Exodus 21:22-25 NAS

In this passage, the punishment for destroying a fetus is different from that of taking the life of a person (the mother), hence the fetus is not considered to be a person. Social conservatives obviously disagree with that interpretation. Pro-Choice adherents also believe a woman has a constitutional right to choose what is done to her body, that she, along with her physician, has the exclusive right to determine if she will carry a fetus to term or have it aborted. Again, Pro-Lifers disagree. They do not believe a pregnant woman has the right to abort the fetus because they consider a fetus to be a person. The religious right maintains that the unborn fetus also has constitutional rights.

Clearly, the struggle over abortion rights will not end in the foreseeable future regardless of possible Supreme Court decisions. So, what should Christians, and our country as a whole, do with regard to the abortion issue? The sad fact is that both the religious right and moderate Christians strive for the same thing, a reduced number of abortions, but they go about it in different ways. The primary reason for our nation's high incidence of abortion is the extremely high number of unwanted pregnancies, especially among young single women and teen-age girls. Reducing the number of those unwanted pregnancies would be a giant step forward in reducing the abortion rate in America, but what is the best way of doing that?

The religious right's basic approach is to teach abstinence-only sex education classes to our young people, eliminate government funding for abortions, and eventually make all abortions illegal. Pro-Choice adherents push for more general sex education classes which include birth control instructions and selective distribution of contraceptives, together with counseling of young women contemplating abortions. Unfortunately, neither approach has shown a lot of success. Studies have indicated that abstinence-only sex education programs do not work, and birth control education programs produce minimal results. In essence, values education without changing environments (or cultures) has been ineffective. Our young people's attitudes toward sex are influenced primarily by the environments and cultures in which they live; they respond to what is expected of them. Their behavior is determined to a great extent by the demands of their environments and their perceptions of those expectations.

Changing the environments in which our young people live, together with developing more effective sex education programs, is therefore the key to modifying attitudes toward sex. Such a huge endeavor would require the participation of parents, communities, churches, cities, states, and the federal government. Development of a program of that magnitude is well beyond the scope of our study, so we will not belabor the abortion rights issue as we define Christian priorities most pleasing to God. Suffice to say, resolution of the abortion rights issue in America will require numerous religious and political compromises, as well as judicial clarifications of constitutional concerns.

Euthanasia is another sanctity of life issue of great importance to the religious right. Their primary concern is so-called "mercy killings" wherein a physician, spouse, family member, hospital, or other person assists a terminally ill and helpless individual end his or her life. We have recently witnessed a few high-profile cases in which family members, the religious right, or conservative Republican politicians have attempted to prevent spouses and hospitals from "pulling the plug" on patients who were in vegetable states with no chance of recovery. Those relatively few high-profile cases drew a lot of media attention and provided a forum for social conservatives to express their views on euthanasia.

Like abortion, euthanasia involves both religious concerns and constitutional considerations, so it is unlikely that issue will be resolved in the near future. In addition, medical directives are available for those who desire to make their wishes known in advance. A significant number of moderate Christians disagree with the religious right. They believe it is inhumane to prolong the lives of terminally ill and suffering patients when their families and/or physicians determine the patients should be allowed to die peacefully and naturally. Because of the increasingly widespread use of medical directives and the relatively low incidence of disputed euthanasia, that issue does not seem to be a high-priority concern for a vast majority of our citizens. The attention and work of Christians should thus be directed toward more pressing needs and concerns in our society.

Homosexual rights and gay marriage is another hot-button issue for social conservatives. They consider homosexuality to be a sinful lifestyle, and the religious right cites Scripture to support their position. One Scripture passage cited is found in the Book of Romans in the New Testament, and related passages are included in the Old Testament.

Therefore God gave them over in the sinful desires of their hearts to sexual impurity for the degrading of

their bodies with one another. They exchanged the truth of God for a lie, and worshiped and served created things rather than the Creator---who is forever praised. Amen. Because of this, God gave them over to shameful lusts. Even their women exchanged natural relations for unnatural ones. In the same way the men also abandoned natural relations with women and were inflamed with lust for one another. Men committed indecent acts with other men, and received in themselves the due penalty for their perversion.....Although they know God's righteous decree that those who do such things deserve death, they not only continue to do these very things but also approve of those who practice them.
--Romans 1:24-27,32 NIV

In this passage, homosexual relations seem to be presented as shameful and immoral activities, unnatural for both men and women. We concluded in an earlier chapter of this book that homosexuality is indeed condemned in the Bible, but that interpretation is rejected by some Christians, especially those who are homosexuals. Fundamentalist conservatives look at homosexuality as an acquired lifestyle, whereas the gay and lesbian community and many moderate Christians believe sexual orientation is determined to a great extent by genetics. The medical community has abundant data suggesting genetics and family environment are major factors in determining sexual orientation, but the religious right rejects that data.

Gay marriage is an aspect of homosexual rights which has been particularly controversial. The religious right does not recognize marriage of two individuals of the same sex, including any form of civil union which provides basic spousal benefits. A sizable number of moderate Christians and non-Christians also oppose same-sex marriage, but many do approve of civil unions wherein basic spousal benefits are provided, such as medical insurance, survivor pensions, and community property rights. The religious right maintains that sexual orientation does not qualify for special consideration under the United States Constitution and Bill of Rights. They refuse to categorize sexual orientation with race, gender, and age, which do receive discrimination protection under the Constitution.

Social conservatives claim the Bible presents marriage as an institution, or covenant, between one man and one woman, for the purpose of procreation. One verse of Scripture in the Book of Genesis clarifies their position, and that concept of marriage between one man and one woman is affirmed throughout the Bible.

> For this cause a man shall leave his father and his mother, and shall cleave to his wife; and they shall become one flesh.
> --Genesis 2:24 NAS

Numerous Scripture passages throughout the Bible are consistent with that initial definition of marriage in Genesis, chapter 2, but God's Word is silent with regard to any form of civil union between two individuals of the same sex. Neither does Scripture present sexual orientation as an acquired lifestyle or the result of genetics.

Sexual orientation is both a religious and a moral issue, and it also involves Constitutional rights. Like abortion, homosexual rights is a matter which cannot be clearly resolved in the foreseeable future. Resolution of that thorny issue must also include religious and political compromises, as well as clarification of significant Constitutional concerns. The mixing of religion and politics has added a new and complicated dimension to two of America's most controversial issues, abortion rights and homosexual rights.

It is thus deemed impractical for Christians to place major emphasis on, and devote a great amount of effort toward, resolving the homosexual rights issue. Homosexual rights does not seem to fit into the Jesus agenda, that of ministering to the poor, weak, helpless, and oppressed members of our society.

The use of embryos in stem cell research is an issue which has caused bitter division in both the religious realm and the political realm over the last few years. This relatively new medical research activity has been linked to abortion by the religious right because it involves destruction of embryos. They claim any destruction of embryos, even for use in finding possible cures for dread diseases such as cancer, should be prohibited. Social conservatives equate an embryo to a fetus and thus maintain they should not be destroyed. The religious right seems to ignore the established fact that large numbers of unused frozen embryos are being discarded by fertility clinics, with no benefit to medical research. Those discarded embryos could be used in stem cell research to find possible cures for spinal injuries and dread diseases such as Parkinson and cancer.

Moderate Christians, as well as a significant number of social conservatives, believe those "doomed" embryos in fertility clinics are good candidates for use in stem cell research. Current federal regulations prohibit federal funding of stem cell research using those discarded embryos from fertility clinics, but several states are funding such research. This type of medical research to help the sick in our society certainly belongs in the Jesus agenda, so I believe support for use of embryos from fertility clinics in stem cell research should be a part of the overall Christian agenda.

Prayer in public schools is a religious issue which has divided Christians and our country as a whole. The

116

religious right charges that we have "taken God out of our schools," resulting in widespread immorality and wickedness in our society. Is that a valid claim? We must honestly consider the facts as we look at our nation's history and where we are today. Keep in mind that teacher-led prayer in schools, display of religious symbols in schools, and teaching of Bible stories in the classrooms have become a contentious matter only in the last few decades. Prior to some thirty years ago, at about the time the social conservative movement was initiated, few of our citizens objected to such religious trappings in public schools. For that reason, religion was allowed to be a relatively small part of our public school systems.

So, from the birth of our nation until some thirty years ago, one could rightfully say "God was in our schools." Does that mean America was a more merciful, moral, and just nation all those years? After all, we had the Bible, religion in our public schools, a Constitution, and a Bill of Rights to guide us throughout our nation's history. But, were our Christian forefathers moral and just when they slaughtered large numbers of Native Americans, confiscated their lands, and defaulted on treaty agreements with them? And, what constitutional rights did those early Native Americans enjoy?

Only certain white male owners of land could vote in the early days of our country. Later, most white males were allowed to vote, but it was not until 1920 that white women won the right to vote. African Americans could not vote until after Reconstruction, and even then all kinds of rigged rules and procedures were implemented to prevent most of them from voting. Southern states in particular, those in the so-called Bible belt of America, were most repressive in limiting African American voting. Our white Protestant churches led the way in efforts to suppress African American participation at the polls. Could one honestly claim America was always fair and just in determining who could cast a ballot? Even today, we see evidence of political parties trying to suppress the vote of minority citizens of our country.

White Christian Americans owned slaves until shortly after the Civil War, and that too was during the time God was allowed in our schools. In fact, our largest Protestant denomination, the Southern Baptist Convention, was founded when it broke away from American Baptists over the issue of slavery. Southern Baptists wanted to keep their slaves. Could we classify the cruel and inhuman treatment of those African American slaves as merciful, moral, and just? Furthermore, are any of our citizens abused today, with God out of our schools, to the same extent that black people were mistreated during those times of slavery?

The best-known white supremacist organization in our country since the Civil War is the Ku Klux Klan (KKK), made up of white Protestant males. The KKK, claiming to be a religious entity, was very active in the South during the late-1800s and early-1900s, and its membership was comprised primarily of Christian white males from main-line Protestant churches. Those radical religious thugs terrorized African Americans throughout the deep South. They burned crosses in front of their homes and churches, torched those same homes and churches, lynched black men, raped black women and girls, and wreaked havoc across African American neighborhoods. And, all of that occurred when God was supposedly in our schools. I do not believe we can classify the KKK's treatment of African Americans as moral, compassionate, or just.

We had essentially two justice systems in our nation's early history, one for white people and one for people of color. The judges, attorneys, and juries were all-white, and racism dictated judicial outcomes for legal proceedings involving African Americans. Black people were convicted of crimes they did not commit, white men were found innocent of crimes committed against black people, and African Americans' property was confiscated or stolen through rigged legal proceedings. That judicial oppression of black communities was neither fair nor just, and it took place while God was in our schools' classrooms.

What does America's checkered past tell us about our present? Perhaps it tells us that religious trappings are not as important as what is in our hearts. Our conduct toward others is a reflection of our internal attitudes, biases, desires, and motivations. If we allow the nine internal attributes derived from the Holy Spirit, namely love, joy, peace, patience, kindness, goodness, faithfulness, gentleness, and self-control, to control our lives, our actions toward others will be merciful, moral, and just. State-sponsored prayer, religious symbols, and religious expressions in our public schools are merely external things which have relatively little impact on our vital relationships with others. That conclusion is consistent with New Testament teaching about what God desires of His people, the Church.

Our logical conclusion must be that eliminating state-sponsored prayer in public schools, display of religious symbols in our schools, and religious expressions in the classrooms have not caused the immorality and wickedness permeating our society. Then, what has? Answering that extremely difficult question is beyond the scope of our study; we will leave it to the sociologists to enlighten us on that complex matter. Let me suggest just a few possibilities, however. Mandatory military service (the draft) was discontinued during the Viet Nam War era, relieving our young people of the patriotic obligation to serve our nation. Public television came into existence, exposing our adults and youth to increasing levels of violence, immorality, greed, and self-gratification. Special-interest groups with big money and selfish ambitions gained control of our politicians and our government. Greed and corruption became firmly entrenched in our way of life and in our relationships with one another. As a people, we became more and more self-centered. Could all those things contribute to the decay of our society over the last few decades?

What do social conservatives really mean when they demand prayer and freedom of religious expression in our public schools? Can those prayers, religious symbols, and religious teachings be Jewish, or Hindu, or Islam, or some other religion besides Christianity? No, certainly not. The religious right is actually demanding that their particular brand of religion, Christianity, be taught in our public schools, but that clearly violates the First Amendment to the Constitution. Perhaps a compromise could be reached regarding religious expressions in public schools, provided clear and enforced guidelines were established to prevent pushing any particular religious belief over all others. This is primarily a constitutional concern, one that is unlikely to be resolved in the foreseeable future, so it does not seem to be a high-priority matter for Christians. In addition, it is an issue that does not seem to fit into the Jesus agenda.

Fundamentalist Christians work diligently to allow the Ten Commandments to be posted in public facilities, a religious issue related to prayer in public schools. Such postings have been allowed in numerous public grounds and buildings for many years, with few complaints until some twenty years ago. Posting the Ten Commandments is actually a religious symbol or expression, and it is a matter of little concern for a majority of our citizens, except for the religious right. Consequently, posting the Ten Commandments in public facilities is not deemed to be a high-priority matter for Christians, and it does not seem to belong in the Jesus agenda.

The final religious issue near and dear to the religious right is teaching intelligent design, or creationism, in our public school science classes. They demand the teaching of creationism as a scientific theory, parallel to evolution. Creationism has no scientific basis; it is simply a religious belief based on the Genesis account of creation in the Bible. As a Christian, I believe the Biblical account of creation, as do virtually all Christians. But, is my understanding of creation the same as that of all Christians? Definitely not. Christians have different interpretations of the Genesis account of creation, so whose interpretation would be taught? Evolution is a valid scientific theory based on many years of research, and it is taught as such in our schools' science classes. On the other hand, creationism is a somewhat murky religious belief which does not belong in a science class. This is an issue which does not fit into the Jesus agenda, a ministry of compassion to the downtrodden in our society.

The religious right maintains that America is a Christian nation and that state-sanctioned Christian prayer in public schools, posting the Ten Commandments in public facilities, and teaching creationism in public school science classes should be allowed. Social conservatives overlook key facts, however. First, our population includes a great number of non-Christian citizens, and a significant number of those folks are affiliated with other religions. Jewish, Hindu, Islam, and other non-Christian religions are well represented in our nation. Second, our country is a democracy, but the majority does not always rule. Our Constitution and Bill of Rights preclude the majority from trampling on the rights of the minority, hence the majority cannot impose their religious views and expressions on the minority. And thirdly, our Constitution and Bill of Rights incorporate separation of church and state. That is a practice which has served our nation well for over two hundred years.

Social conservatives devote their attention to specific well-defined issues such as abortion rights, gay marriage, and teaching of creationism in public school science classes. Those are controversial issues which involve theology, Bible interpretation, politics, and constitutional concerns. Moderate Christians pursue a much broader agenda, one which is loosely defined in general terms. Two Scripture passages in the Gospel of Luke provide a basis for the compassionate social ministry agenda of moderate Christians.

He went to Nazareth, where he had been brought up, and on the Sabbath day he went into the synagogue, as was his custom. And he stood up to read. The scroll of the prophet Isaiah was handed to him. Unrolling it, he found the place where it is written: "The Spirit of the Lord is on me, because he has anointed me to preach good news to the poor. He has sent me to proclaim freedom for the prisoners and recovery of sight for the blind, to release the oppressed, to proclaim the year of the Lord's favor." Then he rolled up the scroll, gave it back to the attendant and sat down. The eyes of everyone in the synagogue were fastened on him, and he began by saying to them, "Today this scripture is fulfilled in your hearing."
--Luke 4:16-21 NIV

When the men came to Jesus, they said, "John the Baptist sent us to you to ask, 'Are you the one who was to come, or should we expect someone else?'" At that very time Jesus cured many who had diseases, sicknesses and evil spirits, and gave sight to many who were blind.

So he replied to the messengers, "Go back and report to John what you have seen and heard: The blind receive sight, the lame walk, those who have leprosy are cured, the deaf hear, the dead are raised, and the good news is preached to the poor."
--Luke 7:20-22 NIV

Jesus Christ defined His own mission in these two passages. That Jesus agenda entailed a spiritual and physical ministry to the afflicted and downtrodden people of His day. Moderate Christians believe their calling is to share the Gospel of Jesus Christ with a lost world and to carry on the Jesus agenda of ministry. Unfortunately, the Jesus agenda is quite difficult to define in our complex and politicized society.

Moderate Christians are convinced that pursuit of a compassionate social ministry to the afflicted in our society is much more beneficial, and thus more pleasing to God, than wrangling over theology and following the controversial moral and social agenda of the religious right. The goal of moderate Christians is to bring all Christians together, set aside differences in theology, ideology, and politics, and concentrate on non-controversial ministry concerns. Cooperative work in critical areas where all Christians agree is preferable to fighting over divisive issues with bitter disagreement being the norm. That is the overall approach to social ministry championed by the New Baptist Covenant, and it is one which I believe pleases God.

We concluded in our study of the New Testament in chapter 5 that God is more concerned about our relationships with others than He is about religious trappings. That means we must place a high priority on our attitudes toward others and on ministry to meet the physical needs of the poor, sick, helpless, and oppressed segments of our citizenry. Our task now is to define what that ministry to the afflicted involves. It must include assistance for food, shelter, clothing, medical care, and legal aid for those who cannot help themselves. But, how do environmental issues affect our ministry to the downtrodden? And, what role should government play in meeting those needs? Also, what is the impact of the greed and corruption permeating our society on the weak and helpless in our midst? Those are questions we must address as we define a Jesus agenda for our society today.

Hurricane Katrina exposed the abject poverty and hopelessness which abound in America, especially in our larger cities like New Orleans. We find poverty-stricken pockets of people in all our cities, all along our border with Mexico, in many rural areas of our country, in ghettos all across our nation, and in many neighborhoods surrounding dying manufacturing and mining operations. So-called "nicer" neighborhoods are not immune to poverty and hopelessness. Scattered among what is considered to be well-off families are senior citizens struggling to survive on very low fixed incomes, sick and handicapped people with extremely limited means of support, single-parent families with grossly inadequate incomes to provide the basic necessities of life, and the chronic unemployed lacking sufficient job skills. Millions of our citizens live in a self-perpetuating welfare culture with little means or motivation to escape from their downward spiral. For the most part, these poor and powerless people are the forgotten masses in America. They are under the radar.

Some help is available for the poor and powerless people in our midst, but it has been insufficient to alleviate the problem. We have various kinds of federal and state welfare programs in place, but they are plagued with bureaucratic red tape, inefficiencies, fraud, and corruption. Various charities, churches, and individual givers provide limited relief, but they lack the resources to meet the needs of such a huge number of poor and helpless people. Because of the magnitude of the problem, our state and federal governments must be involved, and they must bear a major portion of the costs. Poor and afflicted people in our midst need help in two ways. First, they need aid to provide the basic necessities of life, including food, shelter, clothing, and adequate health care. Second, they require help to escape the culture of poverty in which they are entrapped. The state of perpetual welfare we see today must be ended.

Moderate Christians champion a ministry of compassion and justice to the afflicted in our society, as opposed to an agenda which divides and judges our people. But what does that ministry entail? Definition of such a huge and complex endeavor is well beyond the scope of our study, but it requires cooperation between churches, charities, local and state governments, and the federal government. Such a ministry must involve assistance and ministry to specific individuals and people groups by churches and charities. It also requires state and federal programs to provide aid and assistance to broad segments of our population. Politics and ideology must be set aside if such a giant undertaking is to be successful.

The logical, and perhaps the most effective, way Christians can participate in such a large endeavor is through cooperative work by a number of religious entities. Joint efforts by local churches, denominations, and other religious organizations could provide maximum efficiency in reaching large numbers of people with diverse needs. Cooperation with government agencies and private charities must also be an integral part of the overall effort. Any activity requiring state or federal government participation involves politics to some extent, thus it is extremely important that the overall undertaking be bipartisan. That precludes consideration of the divisive moral and social issues which have dominated our nation's politics during the last few years. The New Baptist Covenant, now in the early planning stage, appears to be the type of cooperative effort necessary to have a large impact on poverty and hopelessness in America and around the world.

A lot of Christians are generous in giving personally to charitable causes but maintain the government is not responsible for helping people in need. Those charitable believers provide meals for the homeless, contribute to food pantries, adopt needy families at Christmas time, contribute to the Salvation Army, go on ministry mission trips to poverty-stricken areas, donate goods to poor people, and participate in all kinds of personal charity giving. All that is admirable and beneficial, but those good Christian folks do not realize that what is most helpful to the poor and downtrodden is steady and ongoing assistance, together with measures to help them help themselves. Those unfortunate citizens are in desperate need of the means to escape the environment of poverty and hopelessness in which they are mired.

Government assistance programs such as Head Start, subsidized housing, Children's Health Insurance Program, food stamps, Medicaid, food pantries, and Meals on Wheels are necessary and good, but more is needed to lift the masses of hopeless people out of poverty. They need better education opportunities, more effective and broadly available job training programs, treatment facilities for alcohol and drug addiction, practical sex education and birth control classes, legal aid and legal counseling, transportation and child care assistance, and other such programs to help them become more productive and more self-sufficient. All of those are very large undertakings, and only the federal government has the resources to fund such an endeavor. Charities, churches, and individuals can help administer those government programs for the poor, but funding must be at the state and federal level. Control of fraud and corruption has to be an integral part of each government aid program if they are to be most effective in targeting the truly needy in our society.

Many Christians maintain the Bible does not teach that the government is responsible for helping the poor and powerless in our society. They claim that Scripture passages pertaining to such help are directed to individuals, families, and churches rather than the government. Several of the Scripture passages we reviewed in the Old Testament admonished wealthy people, religious leaders, judges, government officials, and other people of power to help and stand up for the downtrodden people in their midst. Jesus also tells us in the New Testament that the principles for living presented in the Old Testament still apply today.

Learn to do right! Seek justice, encourage the oppressed. Defend the cause of the fatherless, plead the case of the widow.
--Isaiah 1:17 NIV

Woe to those who make unjust laws, to those who issue oppressive decrees, to deprive the poor of their rights and withhold justice from the oppressed of my people, making widows their prey and robbing the fatherless.
--Isaiah 10:1-2 NIV

Hear this, you leaders of the house of Jacob, you rulers of the house of Israel, who despise justice and distort all that is right; who build Zion with bloodshed, and Jerusalem with wickedness. Her leaders judge for a bribe, her priests teach for a price, and her prophets tell fortunes for money. Yet they lean upon the LORD and say, "Is not the LORD among us? No disaster will come upon us."

--Micah 3:9-11 NIV

Now when he saw the crowds, he went up on a mountainside and sat down. His disciples came to him, and he began to teach them, saying:.... "Do not think that I have come to abolish the Law or the Prophets; I have not come to abolish them but to fulfill them."
--Matthew 5:1-2,17 NIV

Numerous other Bible passages reiterate those clear instructions and commandments to help those people who cannot help themselves and to refrain from oppressing the poor and helpless in our society. So, when God's Word commands us to look out for and stand up for the powerless in our midst, I believe those instructions are directed to everyone, including individuals, families, churches, local governments, state governments, and the federal government. If writers of both the Old Testament and the New Testament meant to exclude the government from that responsibility, I believe they would have said so. Unquestionably, assistance to the poor, sick, helpless, and oppressed people in our society belongs in the Jesus agenda, and it must be a high priority matter for Christians today.

Environmental issues have not been a major concern for the majority of our citizens until the last two decades. Haze, smog, and bad odors were the primary problems with air quality, and those were local or regional issues for the most part. Pollution of our lakes, rivers, and coastal waters was also limited to relatively small areas of our country, and thus gained little national attention. Erosion and pollution of our soil did not directly affect a majority of our population, so those issues were not high on the priority list for most folks. Environmental matters were therefore important to only a small percentage of our citizenry and to environmentalists who have always been concerned about abuse and misuse of the environment.

Moderate Christians, as well as a large number of unbelievers and social conservatives, are becoming more and more worried about environmental pollution. Global warming is now a worldwide concern and has become a controversial political topic in America over the last ten years. The Republican Party and the religious right have consistently denied the reality and significance of global warming, especially with regard to human-generated gasses. The Democratic Party and environmentalists agree with a majority in the scientific community who warn that global warming is becoming increasingly more severe and that it is caused to a large extent by human-generated gasses. Scientific reports predict catastrophic climate changes in the not-too-distant future if global warming is not checked.

Industrial pollution, together with the pollution produced by the automobiles and trucks we drive, account for a significant portion of the global warming we are experiencing. Mining companies, the oil industry, petrochemical plants, manufacturing companies, and factories spew pollutants into the atmosphere, poisoning the air we breathe and contributing to global warming. Those same industrial businesses discharge poisonous chemicals into our lakes, streams, and rivers, thus polluting the water we drink. Land developers, timber companies, and the oil industry poison our land, deface our pristine parks and forests, destroy or alter wildlife sanctuaries, and cause flooding and fire control problems around our cities. All those businesses are more concerned with bottom-line profits than they are with the effects of their operations on the environment.

The account of creation in the Book of Genesis, chapter 1, tells us that God gave humankind dominion over all His creation. That means humans are responsible for preserving, maintaining, and taking care of the earth and all of its creatures and resources.

> And God created man in His own image, in the image of God He created him; male and female He created them. And God blessed them; and God said to them, "Be fruitful and multiply, and fill the earth, and subdue it; and rule over the fish of the sea and over the birds of the sky, and over every living thing that moves on the earth." Then God said, "Behold, I have given you every plant yielding seed that is on the surface of the earth, and every tree which has fruit yielding seed; it shall be food for you; and to every beast of the earth and to every bird of the sky and to every thing that moves on the earth which has life, I have given every green plant for food"; and it was so.
> --Genesis 1:27-30 NAS

We can subdue all creatures of the air, land, and sea and use them for our benefit, but we are not to exploit them or destroy them maliciously. The earth's resources are provided for humankind to develop and use for the benefit of both humans and the other creatures of the earth. However, we must preserve the earth's natural beauty, we dare not waste its resources, and we must not pollute its air, water, and land.

How do environmental issues relate to the Jesus agenda, a ministry to the downtrodden segments of our population? Abuse and misuse of the earth and its resources affects everyone. However, the poor, sick, and powerless in our society suffer disproportionately. Power generating plants, refineries, factories, and other industrial operations are quite often located adjacent to low-income neighborhoods, so those unfortunate folks are exposed to the air, land, and water pollution generated by all those industrial businesses. Also, our ghettos and many low-income neighborhoods are concentrated around large cities where air pollution and water pollution are more severe. Poor and disadvantaged citizens have very little political clout, so they are powerless to keep polluting businesses out of their neighborhoods and force state and federal governments to reduce land and water pollution where they live. Poor people do not have access to adequate health care, so they suffer the consequences of illnesses stemming from environmental pollution.

Ordinances, laws, and regulations must be developed to protect the environment, and that involves local, state, and federal governments. Those laws and regulations must be strictly enforced, environmental pollution must be closely monitored, and polluting businesses must be dealt with. Controlling environmental pollution and minimizing global warming is a huge task. It involves every segment of our society, and is an issue that moderate Christians must be engaged in. Protection of the environment does belong in the Jesus agenda.

Greed, fraud, and corruption permeate our society today, and much of it affects the poor and helpless people in our midst. As we discussed previously, greedy corporations pollute our air, water, and land, causing various kinds of illnesses and suffering among people living near those operations. The health and well-being of our citizens are sacrificed at the altar of corporate profits. A large number of unqualified people fraudulently take advantage of government aid programs, thus depriving the truly needy of the help they desperately need. Unscrupulous administrators of government aid programs, both individuals and companies, rake off millions of dollars for themselves and their friends, again depriving deserving aid recipients of the help they need. Corrupt politicians pass laws, implement regulations, and utilize no-bid contracts to funnel millions of dollars of government aid funds to the special-interest groups who contribute to their reelection campaigns. This again reduces the amount of money available for the truly needy.

The list of ways government aid funds are fraudulently siphoned off to undeserving recipients is endless, but the bottom line is that the amount of money actually reaching the truly needy is grossly inadequate. Laws and regulations must be strengthened, loopholes must be closed, oversight must be increased, and qualifications of aid recipients must be verified. Then, government aid programs can get more bang for the buck, and the poor and needy in our society can get the help they need. If necessary, funding for government aid programs must be increased. Charities, churches, and individual Christians must be involved in both private and government programs to help the downtrodden in our midst. That is a work that certainly belongs in the Jesus agenda.

America is afflicted by a number of moral and social ills spread over all economic levels and social classes of our people. Drug addiction and alcohol addiction weigh heavily on the well-being of our nation. Because of that widespread chemical substance abuse by some of our citizens, individual lives are ruined, families are destroyed, lives are lost, crime is rampant, our prisons and jails are full, worker productivity is reduced, property damage is great, healthcare costs are soaring, and the overall financial impact on our economy is huge. Those are not problems for the religious right or for moderate Christians; they are problems for all Americans. The end results for drug addiction and alcohol addiction are similar, but the two issues are quite different. Any use of illegal narcotics is a criminal activity subject to state and federal laws, whereas moderate use of alcohol is not a criminal activity. Alcohol use and narcotics use are quite often related, but excessive use of illegal narcotics represents a much greater challenge to our country.

Partaking of alcoholic beverages is a legal but potentially harmful activity which is somewhat similar to gambling, use of nicotine products, overeating (gluttony), and other such legal but potentially harmful activities. A number of those issues are addressed with passion by various Christian entities whose members harbor strong beliefs about them, but those matters are neither religious right issues nor moderate Christian concerns. The entities deeply concerned about those issues are comprised of Christians from across the religious spectrum. For that reason, a separate chapter of this book is devoted to the use of alcohol. The problem of obesity is also discussed in that chapter.

Helping people enslaved by illegal narcotics, as well as family members affected by their drug addiction, belongs in the Jesus agenda. Individual Christians and our churches must be involved in reducing the incidence of drug addiction and in rehabilitation of those poor souls who are in bondage to that terrible "demon." Christian works in that area can be in many forms, some in the religious realm, others in the private domain, and still others through participation in government aid programs. Drug addiction leads to poverty, helplessness, and hopelessness. Therefore reducing the incidence of enslavement to drugs is a common thread in many of the social ministry concerns championed by moderate Christians.

Widespread marriage infidelity and high divorce rates are two other issues affecting people from all social classes, economic levels, and Christian religions. Surveys show that Christians are just as likely as non-Christians to be divorced, and that includes both social conservatives and moderate Christians. Those in the religious right contend that gay marriages will destroy conventional marriages and families. They can look in their own ranks, however, and see that is not a valid claim. America has experienced only a handful of gay marriages, yet marriage infidelity and divorce rates remain high for Christians professing allegiance to the Christian Coalition. Consider also the number of social conservative Congressmen, presidential candidates, talk radio hosts, church leaders, political candidates, and other prominent individuals who are divorced and/or have been caught in adulterous relationships. And, the religious right is not immune to sexual abuse of minors by church staff. Can all those problems shared by social conservatives be rightfully blamed on gay marriage? I do not believe so.

All Christians should be concerned about marriage infidelity and divorce among their members, but is that an issue which merits high priority in the Jesus agenda? It does involve ministry to the poor and helpless in our society in some instances, but as a general rule that is not the case. It is my opinion that classes addressing marriage, strengthening of families, and divorce prevention should be ongoing activities in all churches.

Thus far we have discussed issues and activities which belong in the Jesus agenda, the Bible's social ministry priorities for Christians. Another extremely important factor is our attitude toward others as we go about those ministries. We certainly must allow the fruit of the Spirit, those nine internal attributes, to be manifested through us as we address the social ills afflicting our nation. It is of equal importance to "put off" bad attitudes, biases, and motivations detrimental to our relationships with others. We must not show favoritism, or partiality. We must not display an attitude of self-righteousness. And, we must refrain from condemning and judging others.

The Bible tells us over and over to stand up for and help those who cannot help themselves. That is the primary thrust of the Jesus agenda we have defined. But, does the Bible's commands to us to help others include mandates for us to change others? Two passages of Scripture from the

Old Testament and the New Testament shed some light on that question.

> With what shall I come before the LORD and bow down before the exalted God? Shall I come before him with burnt offerings, with calves a year old? Will the LORD be pleased with thousands of rams, with ten thousand rivers of oil? Shall I offer my firstborn for my transgressions, the fruit of my body for the sin of my soul? He has showed you, O man, what is good. And what does the LORD require of you? To act justly and to love mercy and to walk humbly with your God.
> --Micah 6:6-8 NIV

> Religion that God our Father accepts as pure and faultless is this: to look after orphans and widows in their distress and to keep oneself from being polluted by the world.
> --James 1:27 NIV

The passage in Micah, chapter 6, summarizes what God expected from His chosen people, Israel, and I believe it also applies to God's people today, His Church. The passage in James, chapter 1, defines pure and faultless religion, what God expects from all Christians. Note that changing others is not incorporated into either passage. If God intended for us to change others, I believe He would have told us so.

Who does have the responsibility to change others if it is not ours? The answer is the One who has the power and authority to do so, our Almighty God. Only God has the knowledge, wisdom, power, and authority to truly change someone. But, God oftentimes uses His people to bring about changes in others, and what we say or do certainly has an influence on people we come in contact with. Our responsibility is to be obedient to God's Word, to witness and minister to people to the best of our ability in Jesus' name, and to trust God to change people in whatever way He chooses. An odd thing happens to us though when we obediently follow the Holy Spirit's guidance to minister to others. God changes us!

The way we live our lives has a much greater influence on those around us than we realize. We share the Gospel of Jesus Christ with unsaved people by means of our verbal witness, but we can also "preach" the Gospel to others by living our lives the way God desires. How we relate to one another, to Christians and non-Christians alike, has a significant impact on those around us. A Scripture passage in the Gospel of Matthew clarifies Christians' role in society.

> "You are the salt of the earth. But if the salt looses its saltiness, how can it be made salty again? It is no longer good for anything, except to be thrown out and trampled by men. "You are the light of the world. A city on a hill cannot be hidden. Neither do people light a lamp and put it under a bowl. Instead they put it on its stand, and it gives light to everyone in the house. In the same way, let your light shine before men, that they may see your good deeds and praise your Father in heaven."
> --Matthew 5:13-16 NIV

Our words and actions must be such that we have a positive influence on those around us, especially unbelievers. People turn away from God and from organized religion when they see pious self-righteous Christians condemning and judging others or ignoring the dire needs of the poor, sick, and powerless in their midst. On the other hand, people are drawn to God and to His Church when they observe faithful Christians displaying love, mercy, compassion, justice, and forgiveness in their relationships with others. Tending to the sick, feeding the hungry, comforting the hurting, helping the helpless, and encouraging the hopeless by Christians are powerful witnesses to Jesus Christ's love for humankind. So, the Jesus agenda is both a ministry to the afflicted and a witness to the unsaved.

Jesus Christ is our perfect example of how we should live our lives and relate to people. Jesus was in the business of meeting needs, both physical and spiritual. Jesus met obvious physical needs in performing the miracles recorded in the New Testament, but the primary purpose of His miracles was to demonstrate God's power and meet spiritual needs of people.

> One day as he was teaching, Pharisees and teachers of the law, who had come from every village of Galilee and from Judea and Jerusalem, were sitting there. And the power of the Lord was present for him to heal the sick. Some men came carrying a paralytic on a mat and tried to take him into the house to lay him before Jesus. When they could not find a way to do this because of the crowd, they went up on the roof and lowered him on his mat through the tiles into the middle of the crowd, right in front of Jesus. When Jesus saw their faith, he said, "Friend, your sins are forgiven." The Pharisees and the teachers of the law began thinking to themselves, "Who is this fellow who speaks blasphemy? Who can forgive sins but God alone?" Jesus knew what they were thinking and asked, "Why are you thinking these things in your hearts? Which is easier: to say, 'Your sins are forgiven,' or to say, 'Get up and walk'? But that you may know that the Son of Man has authority on earth to forgive sins...." He said to the paralyzed man, "I tell you, get up, take your mat and go home."

Immediately he stood up in front of them, took what he had been lying on and went home praising God. Everyone was amazed and gave praise to God. They were filled with awe and said, "We have seen remarkable things today."
--Luke 5:17-26 NIV

When Jesus came into Peter's house, he saw Peter's mother-in-law lying in bed with a fever. He touched her hand and the fever left her, and she got up and began to wait on him. When evening came, many who were demon-possessed were brought to him, and he drove out the spirits with a word and healed all the sick. This was to fulfill what was spoken through the prophet Isaiah: "He took up our infirmities and carried our diseases."
--Matthew 8:14-17 NIV

Jesus did many other miraculous signs in the presence of his disciples, which are not recorded in this book. But these are written that you may believe that Jesus is the Christ, the Son of God, and that by believing you may have life in his name.
--John 20:30-31 NIV

In the passage in Luke, chapter 5, Jesus met a physical need; He healed the paralytic man. In doing so, Jesus demonstrated His power and authority to heal the afflicted and to forgive sins. We see in Matthew, chapter 8, Jesus healing Peter's mother-in-law, demon-possessed people, and others that were sick. Those miracles demonstrated Jesus' power to heal, His authority over evil spirits, and His fulfillment of Old Testament prophecy regarding the Messiah. The passage in John, chapter 20, states clearly the purpose of Jesus' miracles. The physical healing in those miracles demonstrates God's power, that Jesus is the Son of God, and that those believing in Jesus can have eternal life. Christian ministry today must also involve meeting both physical and spiritual needs, following the Jesus agenda.

Chapter 8

Is Moderate Drinking A Sin?

The use of alcoholic beverages, or drinking, is not a candidate issue for the Jesus agenda, but it is a matter of great concern for many Christians. Both social conservatives and moderate Christians have diverse views regarding the use of alcohol, so it has not been a political issue in America. Alcohol use is primarily a concern for individual Christians, some local churches, and a number of denominations. Some Protestant denominations hold strong beliefs about drinking alcoholic beverages, but for others it is a non-issue. A large number of sincere and dedicated Christians believe consumption of an alcoholic drink is wrong, but other equally sincere Christians are convinced that moderate drinking does not constitute a sin. Those conflicting views and convictions have resulted in disharmony, judgmental attitudes, and division within the Christian community.

Our focus in this study is on the attitudes Christians exhibit toward one another regarding drinking, as well as the witness their attitudes present to those outside the Church. Can it be that limited use of alcohol is wrong for some believers, but is not a sin for other believers? And, must we accept and respect the beliefs of other Christians on this controversial issue, even if their views are quite different from ours? It is my opinion that those crucial questions have not been adequately addressed in Bible commentaries and Bible studies pertaining to drinking alcoholic beverages.

It appears that most studies dealing with the use of alcohol incorporate selected Bible passages and interpret them in such a way to justify preconceived convictions regarding that contentious issue. I find that many Christians who deem moderate use of alcohol a sin seem to justify their position by selecting and interpreting Scripture passages in a way to support their established views. That concerns me because I maintain that Bible study should be undertaken to help develop and shape our beliefs regarding important issues of life, rather than to justify preconceived views and convictions. Let us look into God's Word to determine what the Bible does teach about alcohol use. You the reader will find my conclusions to be quite different from those found elsewhere, but I believe mine are based on sound interpretation of Scripture.

Our objective is not to convince any person to abstain from alcohol use or to drink in moderation. Instead, our purpose is twofold. My first goal is to help the readers gain a better understanding of what the Bible has to say with regard to consumption of alcoholic beverages. My second objective is to enable Christians to develop an appreciation for, and a more loving acceptance of, those who have different beliefs and practices pertaining to alcohol use.

Successfully achieving those two goals will help reduce the animosity and division among believers due to their conflicting beliefs about drinking in moderation. That, in turn, will help the Christian community as a whole be more effective in communicating the Gospel of Jesus Christ and ministering in His name. That, I believe, is the desire of all Christians.

Use of alcoholic beverages is presented in numerous Bible passages, most often referred to as wine. Interpretation and application of those Scripture passages to our lives and lifestyles is a major point of contention for many Christians, as well as for a lot of non-Christians. Few issues cause more heated disputes and divisions in the Christian realm than the use of alcoholic beverages. Ongoing debates and arguments over alcohol use are certainly not limited to the Christian community, but our study focuses on how different Christians view Bible teachings on that contentious issue. Amazingly, dedicated Bible scholars often read what appear to be simple and straightforward Scripture passages pertaining to alcohol use but develop contradictory conclusions and beliefs regarding what the Bible teaches about that matter. Hopefully, the study conclusions reached herein will clarify to some extent that murky area of Christian faith.

A number of pertinent questions and considerations are addressed regarding the use of alcoholic beverages. The first thing we consider is what the Scriptures have to say about any addiction, including that of alcohol. We are imperfect and inherently weak human beings, hence it is quite easy for us to become addicted to something we deem sinful, such as illegal narcotics or gambling. But, we can just as easily become addicted to something else we consider good, for example food or work. Our society is full of gluttons and people enslaved by their jobs, as well as drug addicts and compulsive gamblers. Second, we review some of the reasons, Biblical and otherwise, why a large number of Christians choose to abstain from the use of alcohol. Our list of reasons for abstinence from alcoholic beverages is not exhaustive, but I believe it includes the four primary factors influencing Christians' decisions to forego consumption of alcoholic drinks. Two of those factors are based on personal interpretations of the Bible, whereas the other two are not.

Third, we find out if the Bible ever presents the use of alcohol in a positive sense. Excessive use of alcohol is clearly condemned in Scripture, and the Bible points out the potential danger of drinking in moderation; even moderate use of alcohol sometimes leads to addiction. But, does the Bible ever present drinking wine as a normal activity or a blessing from God? Our study addresses that question. Fourth, we determine if drinking is treated as a black and white issue in Scripture or if it is addressed as a grey area. Quite simply, is moderate consumption of an alcoholic beverage always treated as a sin in the Bible (black), or is it always considered to be acceptable (white)? Or, is moderate use of alcohol classified as a sin for some Christians but treated as acceptable behavior for other Christians; is it a grey area? Our study answers those two key questions.

Our fifth concern relates to how our personal decisions regarding consumption of alcoholic beverages must take into account the impact of our actions on others. Sometimes, an acceptable activity by one person has a negative impact on someone else. For example, a casual smoker, one who is not addicted to nicotine, could light up a cigar in the presence of a recovering nicotine addict, thereby causing that person to resume smoking. In such a scenario, it would certainly be best for the casual smoker to refrain from smoking in the presence of the recovering nicotine addict. Our study explores that sensitive area in great depth. Our sixth concern is our attitudes and actions toward others who have views different from ours regarding alcohol use. We do not always understand the reasons for other people's views and convictions regarding the use of alcohol, so we must not be judgmental and disrespectful toward them because they believe differently. It is imperative that we treat all people with respect, not trying to impose our value system and our will on them. This extremely important concern is addressed at great length in our study.

Finally, our seventh and last consideration is what the Bible has to say about our personal decisions and convictions on the use of alcohol. Key to our personal beliefs and commitments with regard to the use of alcohol are our understanding and convictions pertaining to the first six questions and concerns enumerated above. Our comprehension and interpretation of applicable Bible passages have to be an integral part of the process to develop our personal decisions regarding moderate use of alcohol. Each of us has to decide if moderate drinking is acceptable for us or if it is a sin. Our study guides us to that decision.

This writer certainly does not claim to have the "final answer" as to what God's Word has to say about alcohol use. Hopefully, this study will encourage and motivate you the reader to examine your views and convictions regarding the use of alcohol, and will encourage you to delve into God's Word to obtain a better understanding of what the Scriptures teach about that controversial issue. One of our goals is to develop a more loving and understanding attitude toward those who interpret the Bible differently in this sensitive area. That does not mean we all have to agree. If we agree to disagree in the right spirit, then our dialogue on the issue of alcohol use can be constructive rather than destructive in the Christian community. Achieving that goal will enable Christians to have a much greater and a more positive impact on our society regarding excessive and destructive use of alcohol. Christian influence in our society is minimized when non-believers perceive the Christian community to be rife with bickering and discord over some moral or social issue. People respect Christians more when we treat one another with respect, and as a result our society becomes more receptive to Christian views and influence.

For purposes of this study, we interpret drinking wine in the Bible to mean partaking of an alcoholic beverage. That is, if a person drinks enough wine, he or she becomes intoxicated. We do not attempt to differentiate between the various strengths, or alcohol content, of wine used in the many diverse settings of the Bible. We must realize, however, that the wines used in those Biblical settings did indeed have different alcohol content. Similarly, the alcoholic beverages used today, such as wine, beer, and liquor, have varying percentages of alcohol content. Some believers argue that the wine mentioned in numerous Scripture passages is not really an alcoholic beverage, but is merely grape juice. For example, they maintain that Jesus did not drink real wine with His disciples. On the other hand, they claim the wine referred to elsewhere in the Bible is truly an intoxicating beverage. I believe such contradictory definitions of wine in the Scriptures are invalid. It is simply an erroneous attempt to support preconceived beliefs regarding alcohol use. Our study incorporates a consistent, and I believe valid, definition of wine in the Bible.

Another key point must be clarified at this time. There is a distinction between drinking in excess and moderate, or casual, drinking. The Bible unequivocally condemns abuse of alcohol, but it is not as clear with regard to moderate consumption of alcoholic beverages. Nonetheless, many Christians equate moderate drinking to drinking in excess; to them, any use of alcohol is a sin. We make a clear distinction in this study between excessive drinking and moderate drinking.

Our study contains very little, if any, new information relative to interpretation of individual Bible passages. This writer is in general agreement with a majority of the available Bible commentaries when it comes to interpretation of individual Scripture passages dealing with alcohol use. The differences of opinion occur when all related passages are connected together to develop an overall view of what the Bible has to say about this contentious issue. Alcohol consumption presented in the Bible is carefully considered from several different viewpoints in this study, and we will find our conclusions to be quite different from those of many Bible commentaries and other similar publications. This study represents a new and different look at an old and divisive issue, and it is important for us to approach our study with open minds, allowing the Holy Spirit to guide us as we seek to understand what the Scriptures say about moderate use of alcohol.

God's Word has a lot to say about excessive use of alcohol and addiction to it. The Bible speaks clearly against us allowing any thing or any habit to enslave us. What is the meaning of enslavement, or addiction? Quite simply, it means the loss of our self-control and the surrender, or giving up, of our will to something which controls us. Our desire for that thing we are enslaved to becomes so great we must have it, no matter the cost. Oftentimes it means sacrificing our health, our family, our job or career, our money, our reputation, and/or our self-esteem. Feeding that addiction becomes our top priority in life; we lack the willpower and self-control to break the chains of enslavement. Our value system is compromised as the addiction gains greater control of our life. Actions and conduct previously considered unacceptable become the norm for the enslaved person.

What are some of the things to which we can become enslaved or addicted? Such a list surely includes alcoholic beverages, narcotics, tobacco products, gambling, food (gluttony), sex. pornography, wealth, and power, among others. This list could go on and on. Addictions manifest themselves in various ways, some very evident and others more subtle. We easily recognize the person severely addicted to alcohol or narcotics. Their physical appearance, demeanor, and manner of speech are definite signs of their addiction. On the other hand, someone enslaved to gambling or pornography can appear to be quite normal. A parent or even a spouse oftentimes fails to detect a person's addiction to pornography or gambling.

All of us sometimes allow ourselves to become addicted to, or enslaved by, various things, and when we do so we are sinning. God's Word warns us repeatedly about allowing something to enslave us, and the Scriptures tell us enslavement constitutes sin.

> This righteousness from God comes through faith in Jesus Christ to all who believe. There is no difference, for all have sinned and fall short of the glory of God, and are justified freely by his grace through the redemption that came by Christ Jesus.
> --Romans 3:22-24 NIV

> They answered him, "We are Abraham's descendants and have never been slaves to anyone. How can you say that we shall be set free?" Jesus replied, "I tell you the truth, everyone who sins is a slave to sin."
> --John 8:33-34 NIV

For they mouth empty, boastful words and, by appealing to the lustful desires of sinful human nature, they entice people who are just escaping from those who live in error. They promise them freedom, while they themselves are slaves of depravity---for a man is a slave to whatever has mastered him.
--2 Peter 2:18-19 NIV

Since the fall of man in the Garden of Eden, when Adam and Eve ate the forbidden fruit and thus disobeyed God, all humanity has inherited the nature and an environment inclined to sin. Jesus Himself tells us in John, chapter 8, that anyone who sins is a slave to sin, and Romans, chapter 3, informs us that all have sinned. And, we are told in 2 Peter, chapter 2, that we are slaves to whatever has mastered us. The message in those three Scripture passages is reiterated throughout the New Testament. I believe we can conclude from those three passages that addiction to alcohol is enslavement and that it is a sin.

Numerous Bible passages warn of the dangers associated with excessive use of alcoholic beverages. The Scriptures portray in stark detail the potential harm that can happen to a person who drinks excessively, especially someone who is addicted to alcohol.

Wine is a mocker and beer a brawler; whoever is led astray by them is not wise.
--Proverbs 20:1 NIV

Listen, my son, and be wise, and keep your heart on the right path. Do not join those who drink too much wine or gorge themselves on meat, for drunkards and gluttons become poor, and drowsiness clothes them in rags.
--Proverbs 23:19-21 NIV

> Who has woe? Who has sorrow? Who has strife? Who has complaints? Who has needless bruises? Who has bloodshot eyes? Those who linger over wine, who go to sample bowls of mixed wine. Do not gaze at wine when it is red, when it sparkles in the cup, when it goes down smoothly! In the end it bites like a snake and poisons like a viper.
> --Proverbs 23:29-32 NIV

These passages in Proverbs point out the physical harm, the moral decay, the emotional breakdown, the character degradation, and the personality changes resulting from overindulgence in alcoholic beverages. A similar warning is also issued to gluttons, those who gorge themselves on food. Unmistakably, a wise person does not allow himself or herself to be led astray by alcohol and does not associate with anyone who drinks too much. Alcoholic beverages are deceptive. They can look good, taste good, and make us feel good for a brief period of time, but they are corruptive and destructive when used in excess. Note that these Scripture passages deal with those who drink alcoholic beverages in excess. Certainly, the safest stance toward alcohol use is abstinence from all alcoholic beverages, and thus avoidance of the possibility of being addicted to them. We will address casual use of alcohol shortly, but keep in mind that drinking in excess is not the same as moderate drinking.

A lot of people choose to abstain from any form of alcoholic beverages. That is a stance taken by Christians and non-Christians alike, but our focus is on the reasons believers decide not to drink. A Christian's decision regarding consumption of alcohol can be based on numerous factors, but it seems that a majority of non-drinking believers arrived at their decisions on the basis of one, or a combination, of four factors. Two of those factors involve their knowledge and interpretation of pertinent Scripture passages, together with their family and church traditions regarding alcohol use. The other two factors relate more to non-Biblical knowledge concerning excessive use of alcohol, along with their own experience or their family's experience in the area of alcohol abuse.

Quite a few Christians refrain from drinking because of tradition, either that of their family or that of their church. Some of us were raised in families where it was taught that drinking was wrong, and we were forbidden to drink any form of alcoholic beverage. Our attitudes and practices regarding alcohol use were thus formed and developed in the framework of family traditions. Such family traditions may or may not be based on interpretation of the Bible. Other Christians are influenced by their church's view on drinking; they are taught in and through their churches that any consumption of alcohol is evil. Those people arrive at individual decisions and commitments consistent with their churches' views. Church traditions pertaining to alcohol use are based for the most part on the churches' understanding and interpretation of pertinent Bible passages.

A large number of Christians choose to abstain from drinking alcoholic beverages because of their individual interpretations of Scripture passages addressing alcohol use. Many in that group have studied the Bible in great depth, and they interpret specific passages warning about the dangers and risks of alcohol use to mean total abstinence is required. That particular view appears to be somewhat dependent, however, on preconceived beliefs about the use of alcohol. Perhaps the Bible interpretations of those believers are influenced by other non-Biblical factors, such as family traditions or bad personal experiences with alcohol use. They tend to interpret key Scripture passages in a way to support what they already believe about drinking.

Other believers base their abstinence decisions on their perceptions of what the Bible teaches about drinking, rather than on actual interpretation of related Scripture passages. They simply believe the Bible condemns any consumption of alcoholic beverages although they have not personally searched the Scriptures to find out what the Bible does teach about that controversial issue. Their views and convictions are thus developed with only a superficial knowledge of the Scriptures. Their views are also influenced by other factors which contribute to their preconceived beliefs regarding consumption of alcoholic drinks.

Experience is another factor leading many Christians to decide to abstain from the use of alcoholic beverages. Quite often, someone who has a personal background of excessive drinking or someone who has previously become addicted to alcohol will make a choice or commitment to abstain from any use of alcohol. That decision is based on their knowledge of what alcohol has done, or can do, to them personally. They understand the inherent dangers and risks in their continued use of alcohol, so they wisely choose total abstinence. Those believers are to be commended for taking such a stand. Similarly, some believers refrain from drinking because they have seen the adverse effects of excessive alcohol use on family members or friends. Seeing a spouse, a child, a parent, or another loved one become enslaved to alcohol and then watching their addiction gradually destroy them sometimes turns a person completely against drinking. He or she equates what happened to their loved one or friend to what could happen to them if they consume an alcoholic drink. That is certainly an understandable and a commendable reaction by someone who has witnessed alcohol abuse by a loved one.

Lastly, a significant number of Christians base their decisions to refrain from alcohol use on reason, their knowledge of the potential dangers involved in drinking alcohol. Vast amounts of statistical data and information are available to show how easy it is for a person to become entrapped by alcohol and how destructive it is for someone addicted to it. We are also bombarded by media reports and firsthand accounts of crimes, tragedies, accidents, family breakdowns, career failures, financial disasters, and so forth caused by someone using alcohol in excess. It does not take a genius to conclude that if it happens to someone else it could also happen to them. Abstinence is surely the safest stance toward alcohol use, and it is one which minimizes the possibility of a person becoming enslaved by alcoholic beverages.

For those reasons and others, a large number of Christians choose total abstinence from the use of alcohol. Few would question the wisdom of such a stand on this controversial issue, and everyone should be encouraged to take a similar stand. I am sure there are many other reasons people do not drink, but I believe we have touched on the most common ones. A wise choice would be to abstain from drinking alcoholic beverages, but is moderate drinking a sin? Our study addresses that critical question.

We have looked thus far at Scripture passages which warn of the potential dangers involved in consumption of alcoholic drinks. In those passages, alcohol use was addressed in a negative sense. That is, bad things will happen, or can happen, to us if we drink. But, does the Bible always present the use of alcohol in a negative sense, or does it ever address drinking in a neutral sense, or even with a positive slant? Let us examine a number of pertinent Scripture passages to find an answer for that question.

> A man can do nothing better than to eat and drink and find satisfaction in his work. This too, I see, is from the hand of God, for without him, who can eat or find enjoyment?

--Ecclesiastes 2:24-25 NIV

Go, eat your food with gladness, and drink your wine with a joyful heart, for it is now that God favors what you do.
--Ecclesiastes 9:7 NIV

The Teacher in Ecclesiastes had searched for meaningfulness and satisfaction in life. He had pursued many things in his quest for happiness and fulfillment, but in all of them he had found only meaninglessness and emptiness. He had not found satisfaction and fulfillment in pleasure, possessions, power, wisdom, work, or any of the other things he had pursued. Apart from God, the Teacher found all of man's efforts to be in vain. He found ultimately that only a life lived in God's will has real meaning and true happiness. The writer of Ecclesiastes tells us that when we rely on God, revere Him, live life day by day, and gratefully accept the things God gives us, we will be truly satisfied and will have a meaningful life. That is the theme repeated throughout the Book of Ecclesiastes.

The Teacher tells us to graciously accept our particular lot in life, gratefully enjoy the provisions God gives us, find satisfaction in our work, and enjoy whatever life span God grants us. If we do that, God will look on us with favor. Note in particular that Ecclesiastes, chapter 9, verse 7, does not incorporate a negative connotation with regard to drinking wine. Instead, it presents drinking wine as a blessing from God. The emphasis in Ecclesiastes is not on the kind of work we do or on what we eat and drink. Our attitude toward God and our relationship with Him are of utmost importance, however. Only a life lived in obedience to God's will and in fellowship with Him will yield true happiness and a sense of fulfillment.

The Old Testament presents numerous settings wherein drinking of wine takes place. Our study incorporates a brief look at one of them to determine if the Bible does indeed present the drinking of wine in a positive sense.

> Honor the LORD with your wealth, with the firstfruits of all your crops; then your barns will be filled to overflowing, and your vats will brim over with new wine.
> --Proverbs 3:9-10 NIV

Agriculture was the primary livelihood of Old Testament Israelites, and one of their major crops was grapes, from which wine was made. The Israelites were required to give the priests in the temple the first portion, the tithe, of all they produced each year. When they were obedient in giving that tithe, God would bless them with a bountiful harvest. In this particular instance in Proverbs, chapter 3, a bountiful yield of grapes, and thus wine, is presented as a blessing from God to His people, so it seems that wine is viewed in a positive sense. Again, the emphasis is not on drinking wine; rather, it is on honoring God.

Wine appears to be the beverage of choice at feasts and celebrations during Biblical times. A look at three such occasions in the Old Testament indicates that the Bible is neutral on the drinking of wine with meals and celebrations. The three Old Testament passages neither condemn nor endorse moderate consumption of wine.

> Then Melchizedek king of Salem brought out bread and wine. He was priest of God Most High, and he blessed Abram, saying, "Blessed be Abram by God Most High, Creator of heaven and earth."
> --Genesis 14:18-19 NIV

Then he said, "My son, bring me some of your game to eat, so that I may give you my blessing." Jacob brought it to him and he ate; and he brought some wine and he drank.
--Genesis 27:25 NIV

Wine was served in goblets of gold, each one different from the other, and the royal wine was abundant, in keeping with the king's liberality. By the king's command each guest was allowed to drink in his own way, for the king instructed all the wine stewards to serve each man what he wished.
--Esther 1:7-8 NIV

Consumption of wine in these passages is merely a reflection of the practices and customs during those time periods when wine was the beverage of choice. On each occasion described in these passages, the Scriptures state clearly that wine was consumed, but drinking wine was not the primary emphasis in the passages. These examples are only a few of numerous Scripture passages where it appears the Bible is neutral on consumption of wine.

Some Bible scholars admit that wine was consumed on many occasions in Old Testament times, but they maintain that drinking of wine is prohibited in the New Testament. I believe such assertions are erroneous because those scholars equate drinking in moderation to drinking in excess. The New Testament does indeed contain Scripture passages wherein the use of wine is presented in a positive sense. Let us examine two such passages.

Stop drinking only water, and use a little wine because of your stomach and your frequent illnesses.
--1 Timothy 5:23 NIV

This verse is included in the instructions from the Apostle Paul to his protégé, young Timothy. Paul told Timothy to drink wine because of its medicinal value. Reliable medical reports and study results readily available today show the medical benefits of regular but limited consumption of alcoholic beverages. That medical data seems to be consistent with Paul's instructions to Timothy. This verse does not address the issue of excessive drinking or drinking for other reasons. It merely states that partaking of wine would be good for Timothy's health.

The next Scripture passage deals with Jesus' first recorded miracle, turning water into wine at the wedding feast in Cana. It certainly presents consumption of wine in a positive sense.

On the third day a wedding took place at Cana in Galilee. Jesus' mother was there, and Jesus and his disciples had also been invited to the wedding. When the wine was gone, Jesus' mother said to him, "They have no more wine." "Dear woman, why do you involve me?" Jesus replied, "My time has not yet come." His mother said to the servants, "Do whatever he tells you." Nearby stood six stone water jars, the kind used by the Jews for ceremonial washing, each holding from twenty to thirty gallons. Jesus said to the servants, "Fill the jars with water"; so they filled them to the brim. Then he told them, "Now draw some out and take it to the master of the banquet." They did so, and the master of the banquet tasted the water that had been turned into wine. He did not realize where it had come from, though the servants who had drawn the water knew. Then he called the bridegroom aside and said, "Everyone brings out the choice wine first and then the cheaper wine after the guests have had too

much to drink; but you have saved the best till now."
This, the first of his miraculous signs, Jesus performed
in Cana of Galilee. He thus revealed his glory, and his
disciples put their faith in him.
--John 2:1-11 NIV

A wedding feast was a joyous occasion, sometimes lasting
as long as a week. The young couple at Cana could have
been relatives of Mary and Jesus because Mary, Jesus'
mother, was quite concerned about the wine supply being
exhausted. The guests normally drank watered down wine
at such wedding feasts, so presumably Mary, Jesus, and
Jesus' disciples drank the wine along with the other guests.
Excessive drinking was alluded to ("after the guests have
had too much to drink"), but this account of Jesus' first
miracle does not condemn the drinking of wine. Use of
wine is merely presented as a normal and accepted custom at
wedding celebrations during the first century A.D. The
purpose of Jesus' first miracle, turning water into wine, is
the primary focus of the passage. The obvious and
immediate purpose of Jesus' miracle was to satisfy an urgent
need for more wine and thus prevent the family of the
bridegroom from being embarrassed by running out of wine
at the wedding feast. However, the primary purpose of
Jesus' first miracle at Cana is stated in the last verse of the
passage. It was to reveal His glory to His disciples and thus
cause them to put their faith, or trust, in Him.

My conclusion, based on the analyses of the Scripture
passages considered, is that the Bible does at times present
the use of alcoholic beverages in a positive sense. The Bible
does not encourage or condone drinking in those passages
considered, and it does not contradict other Scripture
passages which condemn excessive use of alcohol and warn
of the potential dangers associated with alcohol use. Those
Bible passages and others simply present wine drinking as a

normal and accepted practice in the various settings and time periods of the passages cited.

The Bible is our road map of life. It contains literally hundreds of commands, instructions, warnings, and prohibitions we can follow as we strive to live our lives according to God's will and purpose for us. Those Biblical guidelines address directly or indirectly virtually every issue we are likely to face in life. Numerous questions come to mind as we attempt to interpret the various guidelines and apply them to our lives: (1) Do the commands and instructions in Scripture always apply uniformly to every Christian, or do they sometimes have different meanings for different people? (2) Do Biblical guidelines apply to all believers, or do they ever address only a portion of the Christian community, depending on their particular circumstances? (3) Is it a sin for one Christian to engage in a particular activity, whereas it may not be a sin for another believer to do the same thing? In essence, does the Bible treat all issues of life in a black (bad) and white (good) context, or do some things fall into a grey area? We must find clear and conclusive answers to those critical questions if we are to determine if moderate drinking of an alcoholic beverage is a sin or not.

Let us examine pertinent Scripture passages as we try to answer those key questions about possible grey areas in the Bible. The Apostle Paul refers to grey areas, if they actually exist, as "disputable matters" in the Book of Romans.

Accept him whose faith is weak, without passing judgment on disputable matters. One man's faith allows him to eat everything, but another man, whose faith is weak, eats only vegetables. The man who eats everything must not look down on him who does not, and the man who does not eat everything must not

condemn the man who does, for God has accepted him. Who are you to judge someone else's servant? To his own master he stands or falls. And he will stand, for the Lord is able to make him stand.
--Romans 14:1-4 NIV

This Scripture passage presents a contrast between two types of believers. The first group is comprised of mature Christians, those who have strong faith, and the second group is made up of immature believers, those with weak faith. These definitions of strong and weak Christians are not based on the biological ages of the believers involved, nor are they dependent on the longevity they posses as Christians. These definitions are more of a measure of the faith each group has achieved with regard to the particular issue being considered, in this passage that of Jewish dietary laws and restrictions.

Many early-church Christians were Jews, and legalism carried over from the Jewish religion was a problem within the Roman church, as well as in other early churches. The Jewish religious beliefs included numerous dietary laws and restrictions, and a significant number of the Jewish Christians held on to deep-rooted convictions about what they could or could not eat. Those were the ones Paul considered to have weak faith. On the other hand, those believers with strong faith were secure in their knowledge of the Gospel of Jesus Christ and the realization that Christ had put an end to such religious legalism. They rightly recognized that one's diet has no spiritual significance. Because of their liberty in Christ, the strong Christians did not observe the Jewish dietary laws and restrictions. However, their weak brothers continued to observe the legalistic dietary practices of their former Jewish religion. They failed to recognize that Christ had put an end to such legalism.

Note that Paul did not demand that all Roman believers conform to the same belief and practice with regard to what they could eat. He urged them to accept one another rather than to judge one another, because God had accepted both weak and strong believers alike. The strong Christians were to stop flaunting their liberty and looking down on their weaker brothers who were still clinging to their legalistic Jewish beliefs. Similarly, the immature Christians were to stop judging or criticizing those who did not share their dietary convictions. Paul did not condemn either the strong Christians or the weak Christians. He merely encouraged them to coexist peacefully and accept one another with love and harmony.

Another area of concern for Paul was that of differing views in the Roman church regarding special religious days. Again, many early-church believers had lingering convictions with regard to what was permissible and/or required on the Jewish Sabbath and on other special religious days.

> One man considers one day more sacred than another; another man considers every day alike. Each one should be fully convinced in his own mind. He who regards one day as special, does so to the Lord. He who eats meat, eats to the Lord, for he gives thanks to God; and he who abstains, does so to the Lord and gives thanks to God.
> --Romans 14:5-6 NIV

We see in this passage that the weak Christians considered one day as more sacred than another, but the mature believers considered all days to be alike. The mature believers understood that all days are to be lived for God through a moral lifestyle and in faithful service for Him. Note again that Paul did not require uniformity among the

Roman Christians, and us, concerning observance of special religious days. He does ask us to be steadfast and sincere in our convictions, and he instructs us to honor the Lord in whatever manner we choose to observe special religious days. Paul did not condemn either the weak Christians or the strong Christians for the way in which they observed special religious days. All believers were to honor God in their observance of special religious days, accept one another's differences, and live in harmony serving the Lord.

Paul addressed another divisive issue in his first letter to the church at Corinth. There was disagreement in the church with regard to eating meat which had been sacrificed to pagan idols, or gods. Paul maintained that pagan gods are imaginary, that they are not real gods. There is only one true God, the Father of our Lord Jesus Christ, and all other so-called gods are man-made or imaginary. Pagan gods have no power, and meat sacrificed to them has no spiritual significance. However, that knowledge was not shared by all the believers in the early Corinthian church. Some Corinthian believers still perceived the pagan gods to be real, so to them meat sacrificed to those imaginary gods was of great spiritual significance.

Keep in mind also that the church at Corinth consisted of both Jews and Gentiles. The Gentile believers came from a pagan society, so they were accustomed to worship of pagan gods. They held on to some of the pagan beliefs and practices pertaining to the spiritual significance of eating meat which had been sacrificed to idols and images. A number of the Jewish believers also had strong convictions about not eating meat left over from sacrifices to pagan gods. Paul wrote his letter to the church at Corinth to confront the problems resulting from those differing views of the Corinthian Christians.

So then, about eating food sacrificed to idols: We know that an idol is nothing at all in the world and that there is no God but one. For even if there are so-called gods, whether in heaven or on earth (as indeed there are many "gods" and many "lords"), yet for us there is but one God, the Father, from whom all things came and for whom we live; and there is but one Lord, Jesus Christ, through whom all things came and through whom we live. But not everyone knows this. Some people are still so accustomed to idols that when they eat such food they think of it as having been sacrificed to an idol, and since their conscience is weak, it is defiled. But food does not bring us near to God; we are no worse if we do not eat, and no better if we do. Be careful, however, that the exercise of your freedom does not become a stumbling block to the weak.
--1 Corinthians 8:4-9 NIV

The city of Corinth contained pagan temples where animals were killed and sacrificed to pagan gods. Portions of the animals not used in the sacrifices were eaten by the worshipers or sold to nearby butcher shops. Thus, if a Christian dined with a pagan friend or bought meat at a pagan butcher shop, he was likely to eat meat which had been consecrated to pagan gods. Weaker Christians considered the eating of that meat to be worship of the pagan deity, and therefore a sin against Christ. The more mature believers realized there was no other real God and that meat sacrificed to the imaginary pagan gods had no spiritual significance. Paul did not condemn either group, but he did admonish the strong Christians not to be a stumbling block for their weaker brothers. That could happen if they were seen eating meat which may have been sacrificed to pagan idols. Perhaps the weaker Christians would be tempted to eat the meat which had been sacrificed to an idol even though it was contrary to his or her religious convictions. For him or her, that would constitute a sin.

For each of the three disputable matters addressed by Paul, we find both strong and weak Christians. But, we do not find right believers or wrong believers. Paul merely pointed out that those Christians with a better grasp of the liberty provided through Jesus Christ realized food and drink have no spiritual significance and that one day is no more sacred than another. Those strong Christians were thus free to disregard the dietary restrictions of the Mosaic Law and the observance of special religious days. On the other hand, the weaker believers who did not comprehend the real meaning of religious liberty continued to follow the Jewish religious traditions of dietary restrictions and observance of special religious days. Paul did not chastise either the weak believers or the strong believers. Instead, he admonished all of them to live by their personal convictions, not to judge one another because of different beliefs, and to accept one another in love.

We have considered a few of the disputable matters alluded to by Paul, but there are many other issues which could be categorized into that same grey area. Christians today have diverse views about things such as dancing, engaging in bingo games or other similar forms of gambling, wearing certain types of clothing, wearing makeup or jewelry, working on Sunday, and moderate use of alcohol. We will not attempt to justify the inclusion of any of those activities or others as disputable matters, nor will we attempt to make an exhaustive list of such grey areas. Let us simply conclude that there are numerous grey areas in addition to those explicitly mentioned by Paul. It certainly appears to this writer that the Bible does not address all issues in a black and white context. It is imperative for us to understand clearly Paul's concept of disputable matters before we attempt to determine if moderate use of alcohol is a sin.

Quite a few Bible scholars do not agree with our conclusion that the Scriptures do address some issues as grey areas. They maintain that the Bible presents everything in a black and white context. That is, if it is a sin for one person to participate in a certain activity, then it is also a sin for anyone else to engage in the same activity. To them, a sin is a sin is a sin. I believe such a view is contrary to Paul's teaching about disputable matters. Two Scripture verses, among many others, seem to validate our conclusion that the Bible does allow grey areas.

> One man's faith allows him to eat everything, but another man, whose faith is weak, eats only vegetables.....As one who is in the Lord Jesus, I am fully convinced that no food is unclean in itself. But if anyone regards something as unclean, then for him it is unclean.
> --Romans 14:2,14 NIV

These particular verses pertain to dietary restrictions, but the same truth can be applied to other grey areas as well. Paul states clearly that it is permissible (not a sin) for a believer with strong faith to eat anything. But, eating the same food would be a sin for a weak believer because he considers it to be unclean. So, eating a certain food would not be a sin for one believer, whereas for another believer it would be a sin. The difference is their contradictory perceptions of the spiritual cleanness of the food.

We have considered a number of Bible passages warning against excessive use of alcohol. The addictive and destructive nature of alcohol is portrayed in those Scripture passages, and the potential dangers involved in the use of alcohol are described in vivid detail. Few would question our conclusion that abuse of alcoholic beverages is a sin. That truth is presented throughout both the Old Testament and the New Testament. Our attention now shifts to moderate use of alcohol, or social drinking. Our focus is on Christians who consume nominal amounts of alcoholic drinks, so we will not concern ourselves with either people who are addicted to alcohol or others who overindulge at times. Our goal is to answer a very basic question: "Is it a sin for a Christian to drink a limited amount of an alcoholic beverage?" For clarity, each of us should ask ourselves two personal questions inherent in the above basic question: (1) "Would it be a sin for me to consume a small drink of wine, beer, or liquor?" (2) "Would I consider it a sin if another Christian consumed a small drink of wine, beer, or liquor?" How we answer those two personal questions is of prime importance as we endeavor to interpret and apply the Bible's teaching with regard to moderate use of alcohol.

The first question is quite easy to answer because it deals with our beliefs and convictions regarding our own behavior. Most of us have decided what is right or wrong for us with regard to moderate drinking. We have established limits or conditions to govern our abstinence from, or casual use of, alcoholic drinks. The second question is more difficult to answer. It involves the activities of others, as well as our perceptions of the sinfulness of those activities. Here, we address an extremely touchy matter, that of judging the behavior of someone else. As previously concluded, it is not necessarily a sin for another person to engage in an activity we consider sinful for us. That person's beliefs and convictions may be a lot different from ours on issues which fit into what we refer to as grey areas. We must refrain from trying to impose our beliefs and value system on other people. We have defined Biblical grey areas, or disputable matters, as issues for which Biblical guidelines and instructions may not apply to all people in the same way. For example, it may be a sin for one Christian to do a certain thing, whereas it may not be a sin for another believer to do the same thing.

We build from our discussion of disputable matters as we consider the sinfulness of moderate drinking. Let us examine a key Scripture passage as we try to determine if moderate use of alcohol is indeed a grey area in the Bible.

> I know and am convinced in the Lord Jesus that nothing is unclean in itself; but to him who thinks anything to be unclean, to him it is unclean. For if because of food your brother is hurt, you are no longer walking according to love. Do not destroy with your food him for whom Christ died. Therefore do not let what is for you a good thing be spoken of as evil; for the kingdom of God is not eating and drinking, but righteousness and peace and joy in the Holy Spirit. For he who in this way serves Christ is acceptable to God and approved by men. So then let us pursue the things which make for peace and the building up of one another.
> --Romans 14:14-19 NAS

In this Scripture passage in the Book of Romans, and in others we have reviewed, Paul puts forth five major points. Comprehension and proper application of those five points are vital as we try to determine if moderate use of alcohol is a sin.

First, Paul is dealing with conduct or actions in grey areas wherein Christians legitimately have differing views and convictions. He refers in a more general sense to consumption of food and drink deemed to be spiritually unclean by some people; hence, partaking of such food and drink by those people constitutes a sin. Paul is not alluding to conduct and actions which are clearly and inherently

166

sinful in the light of Scripture. Our decisions in grey areas are guided by our knowledge of the Bible and by our conscience. Keep in mind, though, that Paul does not provide us with an exhaustive list of grey areas; he uses just a few examples to clarify his overall concept of disputable matters. Many other activities or issues could very well qualify as grey areas in the Bible, so our task is to determine if moderate use of alcohol is one of them.

The second point made by Paul is that food and drink in itself is not unclean spiritually. Paul is not addressing issues such as overeating (gluttony), excessive drinking (drunkenness), or violating dietary restrictions resulting from medical conditions or medications. He is talking about beliefs and convictions held by some believers that consumption of certain kinds of food and drink is a sin. Essentially, Paul is saying that food and drink have no spiritual significance. Food and drink are not inherently bad, but our use and/or abuse of them can be a sin.

Thirdly, Paul identifies two kinds of Christians in the Book of Romans. One he refers to as a weak believer, a person who considers it wrong to consume certain kinds of food and drink or to engage in various types of activities which are inherently good. That weak, or immature, Christian could view things such as eating pork, drinking wine, or dancing as sinful. The other kind of Christian is the strong believer, the person who has the Biblical knowledge and mature Christian faith to realize that what one eats or drinks has no spiritual significance. The strong believer also deems it acceptable to engage in activities considered sinful by his immature brother. A word of caution is in order at this time. Each of us is weak at some point in our faith, although we may be strong in others. With regard to grey areas, we must humbly realize that we could be either the strong Christian or the weak Christian, depending on our Biblical knowledge, belief, and conviction pertaining to the specific issue at hand. We must be extremely careful about trying to judge others by imposing our personal beliefs and value systems on them. We may be the weak Christian, the one with inadequate understanding and immature faith, in a particular issue being considered.

Paul's fourth point is that one's belief and conviction about a particular disputable matter should dictate his or her behavior with regard to that issue. For the believer who regards dancing as sinful, it would be a sin for him or her to dance, so he or she should not dance. On the other hand, it would not be a sin for another Christian to dance if he or she considered dancing to be a good and proper activity. The same can be concluded with regard to drinking a glass of wine with a meal. The believer who views any consumption of an alcoholic drink as a sin would be doing wrong if he or she drank a glass of wine, whereas drinking a glass of wine would not be a sin for the Christian who considers moderate drinking to be acceptable. Our knowledge and belief about a particular grey area should determine how we conduct ourselves regarding that issue.

The fifth point made by Paul involves our consideration of others and the impact our actions may have on them. First and foremost, we must always relate to people with love, the same kind of selfless love Christ demonstrated toward us. That love seeks what is best for the other person instead of what pleases self. It may mean sacrifice of our interests in order to do what is best for our neighbor. In other words, we sometimes have to forego our Christian liberty to keep from causing a weaker brother to stumble. When we exercise our Christian liberty in such a manner that we ignore the influence and impact we could have on others, we are not walking in love. We are walking in selfishness instead. Relating to others in love applies to our relationships with unbelievers as well as other Christians. We must not knowingly do anything which would offend an unbeliever or cause them to be further alienated from God.

Paul's primary emphasis does not appear to be on the inherent sinfulness of any particular activity qualifying as a disputable matter. Nor does he seem to place emphasis on his readers attaining a level of understanding and faith necessary to have the liberty to engage in an activity considered to be a grey area. So, what is Paul's primary concern? I believe Paul is concerned primarily about our relationships with one another. Of vital importance to him is our attitude toward, and acceptance of, other believers who hold beliefs and convictions different from us, and our awareness of the impact our actions may have on others. We must strive for harmony with other Christians even when we disagree. We must seek unity of purpose even if we are not uniform in our beliefs, and we must do what is best for the other person even if it calls for sacrifice of our own Christian liberty. Our overall goal must be to minimize the bickering, division, and disharmony within the Christian community resulting from our diverse beliefs and actions related to disputable matters. That, in turn, will increase the effectiveness of Christian churches as we minister and witness in Jesus' name to an unbelieving world.

The Scripture passage considered in Romans, chapter 14, did not explicitly address the issue of drinking alcoholic beverages. Additional verses in that chapter do seem to imply that moderate use of alcohol should be included as a disputable matter. Let us examine those verses.

> Do not destroy the work of God for the sake of food. All food is clean, but it is wrong for a man to eat anything that causes someone else to stumble. It is better not to eat meat or drink wine or do anything else that will cause your brother to fall. So whatever you believe about these things keep between yourself and

God. Blessed is the man who does not condemn himself by what he approves. But the man who has doubts is condemned if he eats, because his eating is not from faith; and everything that does not come from faith is sin.
--Romans 14:20-23 NIV

This passage is a continuation of Paul's instructions about grey areas, or disputable matters. Consumption of wine ("eat meat or drink wine") is included with grey areas, and "these things" obviously refers to all the disputable matters addressed by Paul in the preceding verses. So, our discussions and conclusions pertaining to disputable matters apply to moderate consumption of alcoholic beverages as well. It is thus a sin for a believer to drink if he or she regards use of alcohol as wrong. However, if he or she considers moderate use of alcohol to be acceptable, drinking wine, beer, or liquor in moderate amounts would not be a sin for that believer.

Moderate consumption of alcoholic beverages, or social drinking, can be subdivided into two similar but different forms. One we call public drinking, wherein a person of strong faith consumes an alcoholic beverage in a restaurant, at a reception, at a sporting event, or at some similar public activity. In such settings, a distinct possibility exists for a weak believer who knows that person to observe his stronger Christian brother drinking and thus be led to do so himself even though he perceives use of alcohol to be a sin. Also, an unbeliever could see a person he knows to be a Christian consuming an alcoholic beverage, thereby committing what the unbeliever perceives as a wrongdoing. In either situation, the mature believer's drinking in public could have a negative impact on someone else. I believe Paul cautions us about public drinking because it could possibly be a stumbling block for another person. We do not want a weaker Christian brother to sin because of our actions, nor do we want an unbeliever to be further alienated from God because of something we do. For those mature Christians who drink occasionally, special precautions must be taken to ensure they are not seen doing so by someone who could be led astray or offended.

The second form of moderate alcohol use is private drinking. That involves consumption of alcoholic beverages in the confines of one's home, as a guest of close friends or family members, or in some like setting where the potential risks associated with public drinking do not exist. Many mature believers thus choose to abstain from drinking in public places but do on occasion drink alcoholic beverages in private settings. That certainly seems to be the wisest decision for those who choose to drink socially, and I believe it does take into account Paul's warning about being a stumbling block for another person.

Another interesting point is made by Paul in Romans, chapter 14, verse 22. What we believe about grey areas should be kept between us and God. Strong Christians, those whose mature faith and knowledge give them liberty to engage in activities perceived as sinful by weaker believers, must not flaunt their liberty before their weaker brothers and look down on them. Weaker Christians, those who lack the faith and understanding to have liberty in some grey areas, must also keep their convictions about such matters between themselves and God. Immature Christians must not criticize or judge their stronger brothers for engaging in activities they consider sinful. I believe Paul is telling each of us not to try to force our views and convictions on other Christians, and to respect the beliefs and practices of others. We must recognize the differing beliefs of our Christian brothers, accept them even though we disagree with them, and live in peace and harmony with them. Much of the division and animosity within the

Christian community could be eliminated if every believer would do that.

I believe our conclusions regarding disputable matters are accurate thus far, but I find two verses in the passage we examined in the Book of Romans and a related verse of Scripture in the Book of Colossians to be troubling.

Do not allow what you consider good to be spoken of as evil.....So whatever you believe about these things keep between yourself and God. Blessed is the man who does not condemn himself by what he approves.
--Romans 14:16,22 NIV

Therefore do not let anyone judge you by what you eat or drink, or with regard to a religious festival, a New Moon celebration or a Sabbath day.
--Colossians 2:16 NIV

The precise meaning and application of Romans, chapter 14, verse 16, and the verse in Colossians seems to be somewhat vague. Also, I am not sure how we can reconcile those two verses with Romans, chapter 14, verse 22. Perhaps verse 16 in Romans and verse 16 in Colossians instruct us to keep criticisms of our belief about a particular issue from weakening our convictions on that issue. We must remain strong and steadfast in our convictions in spite of ridicule and criticism from believers who disagree with us. And, maybe we should do so without verbalizing our views to others, thus obeying the instructions in Romans, chapter 14, verse 22, to keep what we believe about disputable matters between us and God. Verbalizing our beliefs about an issue to a weaker Christian quite often increases the disharmony, so perhaps we should be careful about expressing our views on divisive issues.

The Bible contains a number of other Scripture passages relevant to our study of moderate use of alcohol. Let us consider one such passage used in selecting church leaders.

> Deacons, likewise, are to be men worthy of respect, sincere, not indulging in too much wine, and not pursuing dishonest gain.
> --1 Timothy 3:8 NIV

In chapter 3 of his first letter to young Timothy, the Apostle Paul lists the qualifications required of two church leaders, the overseers (bishops, or pastors) and the deacons, and verse 8 is included in the qualifications for deacons. It seems to me that if Paul meant for deacons to refrain from wine he would have said so. To me, "not indulging in much wine" means deacons should never drink excessive amounts of an alcoholic beverage; their drinking should be in moderation. Deacons' decisions to either abstain from alcohol use or drink in moderation should be guided by their individual beliefs and convictions on that issue. Everything the Bible has to say about disputable matters applies to both church leaders and lay Christians.

Definite risks and potential dangers are inherent in even casual use of alcohol. As stated previously, Scripture warns of the addictive and destructive nature of alcohol, so moderate use of alcohol could progress to harmful and excessive drinking. But, do such risks and potential dangers make moderate consumption of an alcoholic beverage a sin? Not necessarily, because I fail to find a firm Biblical correlation between the risk associated with an activity and the sinfulness of that activity. If such a correlation did exist, it would be a sin to engage in high-risk recreational and sports activities such as boxing, automobile racing, mountain climbing, and the like. Similarly, employment in hazardous professions such as law enforcement, space flight, coal mining, and off-shore drilling would be sinful. In essence, we must adhere to what the Bible actually teaches about alcohol use and not try to read our preconceived views and convictions into Scripture. I believe our study has clearly shown that moderate use of alcohol is not a sin if we adhere to the teaching of Paul about disputable matters.

Christians have legitimate disagreements regarding the sinfulness of moderate drinking, but we must not allow those differences of opinion to affect our relationships with one another. Many Christians seem to devote more time and energy crusading against those things they oppose than they do in meeting the needs of the poor and helpless in our society. A large number of believers, and even denominations, are known for the things they are against, rather than the things they are for. Regardless of our different beliefs about moderate drinking, we must set those disagreements aside and carry on the Jesus agenda, that of ministering to the downtrodden in our society.

A Scripture passage in the Book of Proverbs connects excessive drinking , drunkenness, with excessive eating, gluttony. Those are two different addictions, but both are extremely destructive.

> Listen, my son, and be wise, and keep your heart on the right path. Do not join those who drink too much wine or gorge themselves on meat, for drunkards and gluttons become poor, and drowsiness clothes them in rags.
> --Proverbs 23:19-21 NIV

Obesity is one of most pressing health issues faced by our country, especially among our children and youth. Obesity leads to all kinds of health problems, including high blood pressure, diabetes, heart ailments, knee problems, stroke, and numerous others. If not checked, obesity in our nation will lead to millions of premature deaths, force an overload of our health care system, cause a huge number of serious illnesses, reduce productivity in the workplace, cost our country billions of dollars for health care, and reduce the overall quality of life for a large portion of our population.

Addiction to food by our young people could cost America many more lives and dollars than will either nicotine addiction (smoking) or addiction to alcohol. Yet, the Christian community does not seem to be overly concerned about widespread obesity, and they are doing little to alleviate the bad eating habits of our citizenry. I am not sure what role Christians should play in the fight against obesity in our nation, but they must be involved in a significant way. Local churches must join the fight against obesity, and perhaps denominations and alliances similar to the New Baptist Covenant can lead the way.

Many Christians opposed to moderate use of alcohol cite Scripture to support their position. Let us examine two of those cited Bible passages.

> Do you not know that you are a temple of God, and that the Spirit of God dwells in you? If any man destroys the temple of God, God will destroy him, for the temple of God is holy, and that is what you are.
> --1 Corinthians 3:16-17 NAS

> Or do you not know that your body is a temple of the Holy Spirit who is in you, whom you have from God, and that you are not your own? For you have been bought with a price: therefore glorify God in your body.
> --1 Corinthians 6:19-20 NAS

These passages present our body as a temple of God, a residence of the indwelling Holy Spirit. Our bodies are thus holy and should not be defiled or harmed. We find no Biblical evidence suggesting that moderate use of alcohol defiles our bodies, but the passage in Proverbs, chapter 23, shows clearly that overeating does defile our bodies and that gluttony is a sin. In my opinion, the issue of obesity in America should be included somehow in priorities for Christians, the Jesus agenda.

Chapter 9

The Bottom Line

The top priority for all Christians is evangelism, the sharing of the Gospel of Jesus Christ, the Good News, with a lost world. A large part of the New Testament is devoted to growth of the early church and to missionary work of the Apostle Paul, Barnabas, and others. We are instructed throughout the New Testament to share the Good News with those around us.

> Then Jesus came to them and said, "All authority in heaven and on earth has been given to me. Therefore go and make disciples of all nations, baptizing them in the name of the Father and of the Son and of the Holy Spirit, and teaching them to obey everything I have commanded you. And surely I am with you always, to the very end of the age."
> --Matthew 28:18-20 NIV

"But you will receive power when the Holy Spirit
comes on you; and you will be my witnesses in
Jerusalem, and in all Judea and Samaria, and to the
ends of the earth."
--Acts 1:8 NIV

We refer to the passage in Matthew as The Great
Commission, a command to all Christians to lead people to
faith in Jesus Christ, to baptize them, and to teach them how
to serve the Lord. The passage in Acts is a clear directive
for believers to be witnesses for Christ (share the Good
News), starting in our communities and reaching to all parts
of the world.

Christians in America have squabbled bitterly for two
decades over theology, ideology, and controversial moral
and social issues. A number of those issues have entered the
political realm as a result of close ties between the religious
right and the Republican Party. A vast amount of Christian
energy and resources have thus been expended during the
last twenty years fighting political battles. That fighting
among His people cannot be pleasing to God. Many
moderate Christians are concerned about so much "wasted
effort" on the part of individual believers and churches, and
they are seeking a ministry direction less controversial and
more pleasing to God. That is the major thrust of this book,
to define Christian priorities more pleasing to God in the
confines of our politicized society.

We concluded earlier that Christian ministry must be
patterned after our perfect example, our Lord Jesus Christ.
We refer to the social ministry of Christ as the Jesus agenda,
a mission He defined in the Gospel of Luke.

"The Spirit of the Lord is on me, because he has
anointed me to preach good news to the poor. He has
sent me to proclaim freedom for the prisoners and

recovery of sight for the blind, to release the oppressed, to proclaim the year of the Lord's favor."
--Luke 4:18-19 NIV

So he replied to the messengers, "Go back and report to John what you have seen and heard: The blind receive sight, the lame walk, those who have leprosy are cured, the deaf hear, the dead are raised, and the good news is preached to the poor."
--Luke 7:22 NIV

Included in Jesus' mission on earth was physical ministry to the poor, sick, weak, and oppressed people of His day. We therefore made physical ministry to poor, sick, helpless, oppressed, and downtrodden people in our society a high Christian priority. A ministry addressing the social ills afflicting our country also has a tremendous impact on Christians' primary mission, that of spreading the love of Christ and the Gospel of Jesus Christ to a lost world.

We discussed and evaluated numerous candidate issues for our Jesus agenda, a compassionate social ministry to the afflicted in our society. The issues considered include social conservative causes championed by the religious right, matters of primary interest to more moderate Christians, and issues of interest across the entire religious spectrum. A number of issues examined are controversial, involving religion, politics, and constitutional considerations. A majority of the matters included in our Jesus agenda require joint efforts by individual Christians, churches, charities, and government entities, so specific programs, actions, and responsibilities are not spelled out. Nonetheless, I believe we defined Christian priorities consistent with Jesus Christ's definition of His own mission, the Jesus agenda.

Our goal is to set Christians' differences in ideology, theology, and politics aside and concentrate our efforts in areas where we do agree. That means some controversial moral and social issues are not incorporated into our Jesus agenda of ministry. In addition, other issues important to a large number of believers simply do not fit into the Jesus agenda we defined, so those were omitted from consideration. A significant number of Christians obviously disagree with the priorities we established, and they will continue in the ministries and activities they do support. That is well and good because it is important for all believers to participate in Christian endeavors consistent with their beliefs and convictions.

Our society is much more complex than that of Jesus' day, so a social ministry consistent with His mission is difficult to define. The focus of the Jesus agenda we developed is on ministry to needy and helpless people who cannot help themselves, but that ministry involves a number of related issues. Some of those related issues have a direct impact on our social ministry to the afflicted, whereas for others the impact is more indirect. For example, environmental issues affect the poor, sick, and helpless segments of our population both directly and indirectly. Let us now summarize the issues and concerns included in our Jesus agenda, as well as those matters rejected for various reasons.

Christians' top priority after evangelism is compassionate social ministry to the afflicted in our society. That covers a wide range of issues related to helping downtrodden people who cannot help themselves. The afflicted in our society includes those people living in abject poverty, families with insufficient food and shelter, severely handicapped citizens, our homeless population, senior citizens on very low fixed incomes, people with dread diseases such as AIDS, children with inadequate health care, the chronically unemployed, poor people in need of legal counsel, and others with similar hopeless circumstances.

The list of helpless and hopeless people in America goes on and on.

Meeting the physical and material needs of such a multitude of people with a wide range of dire circumstances is a gigantic undertaking. A lot of help is already available from a variety of sources, including individual Christians, churches, charities, local and state governments, and the federal government. But, much more is needed. Two basic kinds of assistance are required for truly needy people; near-term aid to alleviate their immediate intolerable situations, and long-term assistance to help them escape their hopeless circumstances. Unfortunately, most church ministries, charity work, and government aid programs address primarily short-term needs rather than long-term solutions. That simply perpetuates the problems.

Individual Christians, churches, and charities can and should do more to help those unfortunate folks escape from their poverty-stricken and hopeless environment, but their resources are limited. Cooperative efforts by religious entities maximize the impact of the Christian community in helping the needy, but finances required for large aid programs exceed their capabilities. Only the federal government, and to some extent state governments, have the financial clout to make a big difference in the lives of our impoverished and helpless masses. Existing programs must be expanded and made more efficient, and new programs have to be developed. Emphasis in new programs should be on measures to enable downtrodden people to escape from their environments of helplessness and hopelessness.

Government assistance programs should utilize charities, churches, and individual Christians to reach the multitude of needy people efficiently. Rampant fraud and corruption must also be reduced to yield maximum benefit for each dollar of aid. New and innovative approaches for cooperative work by churches and governments have to be developed to enable the Christian community to achieve maximum impact ministering to the social ills in our country. Part of the solution, of course, is for Christians to help elect politicians who will pass laws and establish government assistance programs to help citizens who cannot help themselves. And, to be truly successful, such a huge undertaking has to be bipartisan. It cannot be a Democratic initiative or a Republican initiative.

Many poor people lack education and job skills to earn livable wages. Others are addicted to alcohol or drugs and are thus unfit for gainful employment. Unwanted pregnancies and lack of transportation and childcare prevent a large number of single mothers from entering the job market. Individual Christians and churches are helping those folks as best they can, but only government intervention can truly alleviate those chronic problems and help the masses of unfortunate people rise above their circumstances.

Equal education opportunities must be provided for poorer citizens, job training programs have to be expanded and made more effective, additional and ongoing treatment facilities are needed for alcohol and drug addicts, practical sex education and birth control programs must be developed, and expanded and widely available transportation and childcare assistance is needed for working mothers. Again, Christians and churches must work with federal, state, and local governments to help those who cannot help themselves.

Environmental pollution affects poor and helpless people disproportionately. A majority of our ghettos and many low-income neighborhoods are concentrated near large cities where land, air, and water pollution is more severe. Poisonous chemicals in the air we breathe, the water we drink, and the land on which we walk lead to significant health problems, and a large number of poor people lack adequate health care to treat illnesses resulting from the pollution. Poor people have very little political clout, so they are unable to keep polluting industries out of their neighborhoods or force state and federal governments to control environmental pollution. It is important for Christians to be actively involved in reducing environmental pollution, including the election of politicians who will enact more effective laws and regulations to protect our fragile environment. Environmental causes thus belong in the Jesus agenda.

The use of embryos in government-funded stem cell research is a health issue which has also become a political issue. Stem cell research has the potential to find cures for spinal injuries, cancer, Parkinson disease, and other dread diseases. We concluded previously that discarded embryos from fertility clinics are good candidates for use in government-funded stem cell research. The Jesus agenda includes help for the sick, so Christians should support such medical research programs seeking prevention or cures for major illnesses and injuries.

Widespread obesity is one of the most pressing health issues in our country, and it is the result of eating too much food and/or eating the wrong kinds of food. We find high incidences of obesity in all social and economic levels of our society and in all ethnic people groups. Obesity leads to all kinds of health problems, so it is a matter of concern for Christians. High rates of obesity among our children and youth are especially disturbing because of associated health problems, work limitations, lower life expectancy, and reduced quality of life. I am not sure just what role Christians should have in the fight against obesity, but they must be involved at the local level and in government programs pressing for moderation in our eating habits. The battle against obesity belongs in the Jesus agenda.

We have enumerated those causes included in our Jesus agenda, but what about the issues left out? Abortion, euthanasia, homosexual rights, and gay marriage are extremely controversial moral and social issues which involve religion, politics, and constitutional concerns. We see an ongoing struggle over those hot-button causes, and that fighting will not end in the foreseeable future regardless of future Supreme Court decisions. Christians must set those divisive matters aside and concentrate on more pressing needs we can meet.

Other controversial issues omitted from our Jesus agenda include state-sponsored prayer in public schools, posting the Ten Commandments in public facilities, and teaching creationism in public school science classes. Those matters also involve constitutional considerations, and they too will not be resolved in the foreseeable future. In addition, those three issues represent external religious trappings which have no direct bearing on social ministry to the afflicted in our society. The Apostle Paul tells us to emphasize internal matters, the attitudes displayed in our relationships with others, rather than external matters. Consequently, prayer in public schools, posting the Ten Commandments, and teaching creationism do not belong in our Jesus agenda.

Moderate use of alcohol is an issue of prime importance to some Christians, but we omitted it from our Jesus agenda. Excessive drinking, or alcohol addiction, is a matter of concern for all Christians, and it is included as a part of our compassionate social ministry to the afflicted among us. Moderate use of alcohol is one of the Apostle Paul's disputable matters, so it really is a matter of personal choice for each Christian. Moderate drinking does not cause or change the plight of the poor, weak, oppressed, and helpless, so it does not belong in the Jesus agenda.

Christians' attitude toward the afflicted in our society, as well as toward those we are ministering with, is a key element in our compassionate social ministry. The Bible commands us not to show favoritism, or partiality, toward others. That means we are not to be prejudiced or biased toward anyone because of their race, nationality, religion, social status, or economic station in life. The Scriptures also warn us about being self-righteous. We are not to feel spiritually superior to others and look down on them because of their plight or station in life. Jesus came down hard on the Pharisees, the religious leaders of His day, because of their self-righteousness. He called them hypocrites.

Judgment of others is another attitude we must avoid. We find it very tempting to judge another person because his or her beliefs, value system, or lifestyle may be different from ours. When we judge others, we are attempting to impose our beliefs, value system, and lifestyle on them. We must leave all judgment to God; He alone can judge people. The Apostle Paul tells us to exhibit the fruit of the Spirit, namely love, joy, peace, patience, kindness, goodness, faithfulness, gentleness, and self-control, in our lives. The fruit of the Spirit are nine internal attributes, derived from the indwelling Holy Spirit, which should characterize our relationships with other people. Our compassionate social ministry to the afflicted among us is more effective and more beneficial when we are more Christ-like in our attitudes and actions toward those we are ministering to and toward other Christians we are working with.

Our living witness is dependent to a great extent on the manner in which we perform our ministry to the downtrodden in our society, the way we carry out the Jesus agenda. It is imperative that we allow the love of Christ to be manifested through us as we touch the lives of those unfortunate folks we minister to. Unbelievers' perceptions of God's people, Christians like you and me, determine their responses to our verbal witness of the Gospel of Jesus Christ. As Christians, our actions must match our words. We must walk the talk.

Christians are a diverse family of God, with one faith in one Lord, Jesus Christ, but with many beliefs about a variety of moral and social issues. And, we share one desire, to please God. I challenge each of us to set aside our differences in theology, ideology, and politics and stop spending our time and resources fighting over controversial issues with no foreseeable resolution. Let us concentrate instead on those causes we agree on, and can be most effective in, as we carry out the Jesus agenda. May God bless America as we continue Jesus' mission on earth.

To Order Additional Copies of

PLEASING GOD: THE JESUS AGENDA

Available Through Bookstores

And at:

www.amazon.com

www.barnesandnoble.com

www.borders.com

and others

Printed in the United States
136170LV00003B/43/A